Valuation and Selection
of
Convertible Bonds

Valuation and Selection
of
Convertible Bonds

BASED ON MODERN
OPTION THEORY

Stefaan J. Gepts

PRAEGER

New York
Westport, Connecticut
London

Library of Congress Cataloging-in-Publication Data

Gepts, Stefaan J.
  Valuation and selection of convertible bonds.

  Bibliography: p.
  Includes index.
  1. Convertible bonds.   I. Title.
HG4651.G46   1987   332.63'23   87-14606
ISBN 0-275-92466-1 (alk. paper)

Library of Congress Catalog Card Number: 87-14606
ISBN: 0-275-92466-1

First published in 1987

Praeger Publishers, One Madison Avenue, New York, NY 10010
A division of Greenwood Press, Inc.

Printed in the United States of America

The paper used in this book complies with the Permanent Paper Standard issued by the National Information Standards Organization (Z39.48-1984).

10   9   8   7   6   5   4   3   2   1

Contents

List of Main Symbols

a	Accrued interest
α	Accrual period as a fraction of a coupon period
B, B_c, B_f, B_i, B_n	Total, conversion, floor, intrinsic, and nominal values of a convertible bond in currency units
b, b_c, b_f, b_i	Total, conversion, floor, and intrinsic values of a convertible bond as a fraction of its nominal value
B_c', b_c'	Sum of conversion value and margin payments in currency units, and as a fraction of the nominal bond value
β	Beta value of a stock
C, c, c'	Value of a coupon in currency units, as a fraction of the bond's nominal value, and as a fraction of its redemption value
C_b, C_s	Bond and stock currencies of a convertible Euro-bond
d	Duration of a bond
d_1, d_2	Arguments of the cumulative standardized normal probability distribution in the Black-Scholes valuation formula
Δ	Absolute increase in the value of a parameter
δ_n, δ	Nominal and market conversion exchange rates
E	Exercise price of a regular call option
e_ρ^i	Elasticity of the investment value of a convertible bond with respect to the discount rate ρ

vii

$e^i_{\rho'}$ Elasticity of the investment value of a convertible bond with respect to the discount rate ρ'

e^ρ_r Elasticity of the discount rate ρ with respect to the risk-free rate of interest r

$e^b_r,\ e^i_r,\ e^o_r$ Interest elasticity of the bond value, the investment value, and the option value of a convertible bond

$e^b_s,\ e^i_s,\ e^o_s$ Stock price elasticity of the bond value, the investment value, and the option value of a convertible bond

ϵ Stock exchange rate

f Value function of a call or conversion option

Φ Cumulative standardized normal probability distribution

γ Bond exchange rate

$I,\ i$ Investment value of a convertible bond in currency units, and as a fraction of its nominal value

$I_m,\ i_m$ Investment value of a convertible bond at the time of maturity of its conversion option, in currency units and as a fraction of its nominal value

$I'_m,\ i'_m$ Sum of margin payments and investment value at maturity in currency units, and as a fraction of the nominal bond value

$M,\ m$ Margin or side payments in currency units and as a fraction of the nominal bond value

N The integer number of shares of common stock to be received at conversion

$O,\ O_e,\ O_f,\ O_i,\ O_t$ Total, excess, floor, intrinsic, and time value of the conversion option of a convertible bond in currency units

o, o_e, o_f, o_i, o_t	Total, excess, floor, intrinsic, and time value of the conversion option of a convertible bond as a fraction of its nominal value
o_1, o_2	The two terms in the Black-Scholes formula whose difference equals a bond's option value
p_c	Conversion price
PV	Present value
R_b, R_i, R_o, R_s, R_m	Annualized instantaneous rate of return on a convertible bond, on its straight bond investment, on its conversion option, on its underlying stock, and on the stock market portfolio
$R_\rho, R_r, R_\gamma, R_\delta, R_\epsilon$	Annualized instantaneous rate of change of a bond's discount rate, of the risk-free rate of interest, and of the bond, conversion, and stock exchange rates
R_{o_1}, R_{o_2}	Annualized instantaneous rate of change in o_1 and in o_2
r, r'	Continuously compounded risk-free rate of interest, and its equivalent when interest is compounded once per coupon period
r_c	Conversion ratio
ρ, ρ'	Continuously compounded discount rate that corresponds to a bond's risk-class, and its equivalent when compounding takes place once per coupon period
S	Price of the stock underlying a convertible bond
Σ	Summation operator
σ^2	The volatility of the price of a stock
τ, t	Time to maturity of a convertible bond, and of its conversion option
V, v	Redemption value of a bond in currency units, and as a fraction of its nominal value

x   *List of Main Symbols*

V_o Value per share of a call option

v' Sum of margin payments and redemption value as a fraction of the nominal bond value

Preface

Convertible bonds are hybrid securities that combine straight bond characteristics with a conversion feature. The purpose of this book is to clarify this hybrid nature of convertible bonds and to describe and explain advanced valuation and selection techniques, based on results from straight bond theory on one hand and from stock option theory on the other.

Convertible bonds have been treated as second-rank securities by the investment community for a long time, and have largely been neglected as a subject of analysis and research by the academic community. The lack of interest of the first group may have contributed to the relative indifference of the second, and vice versa. Underlying this common lack of interest, I believe, is the complex nature of these securities, which causes them to be one of the least understood financial instruments currently in use.

Things are changing, however. In recent years, interest in convertible bonds by potential issuers and by the investment community has been growing, as witnessed by the increasing dollar values of new convertible bond issues and by the fast-growing number of convertible bond funds. It is my hope that this work may further stimulate interest in convertible bonds, and contribute to a better understanding of their implications.

The whole text has been written from the investor's point of view, and does not reflect the interests of the issuer of convertible bonds. As investor and issuer are opponents in the convertible bond game, many results in the present text also have implications for the issuer. The discussion of these implications is, however, not within the scope of this work.

Although this book is predominantly analytic in nature, it is in the first place directed to professionals in the world of financial investments who are directly or indirectly involved in bond portfolio management, and to sophisticated individual investors interested in convertible bond investments. In the second place, it is also aimed at readers with an academic interest in the subject of convertible bonds, that is, readers who are more interested in understanding the fundamental relationships underlying the valuation and selection techniques than in using these techniques for practical purposes. Although the analysis of the present text is theoretically well founded, it is at the same time practically oriented in that it offers guidelines to solve the kind of decision problems faced by bond portfolio managers in practice. In this sense, the book can be considered an attempt to bridge the proverbial gap between theory and practice.

An attempt has also been made to present the subject matter in a clear and understandable way without sacrificing scientific rigor. Discussions of irrelevant theoretical aspects and of purely academic issues have been avoided throughout the text. Preliminary knowledge of bond and call option theory is helpful, but not strictly required, to understand the subject matter. All the basic principles of call option valuation are explained in detail in Chapter 3. In addition, more advanced results from option theory as well as a number of results from bond theory are described and explained without mathematical proof. Despite the complicated appearance of certain formulas, all mathematics used in the analysis has been kept as simple as possible, and no familiarity with quantitative techniques beyond elementary algebra is required. To help the reader understand the quantitative concepts and results, numerous numerical examples and a number of graphical illustrations have been included.

A word of thanks is in order to Staf Van Den Bergh, bond portfolio manager at Bank Brussel Lambert in Brussels, with whom I had numerous discussions on current practices in convertible bond management. Furthermore, I want to thank Preston M. Harrington, III, vice president at Merrill Lynch in New York, for providing relevant information on current and past conditions in the convertible bond market. I also thank my colleague at James Madison University, Paul Leidig, for helping me create the graphical illustrations on the computer. And, last but not least, I also owe many thanks to my wife Ann for her technical assistance and all-around support in the realization of this book.

1

Introduction

Although convertible bonds are not as popular an investment vehicle as straight bonds or stocks, potential profits
from investments in them are quite considerable and, if well
selected and managed, they usually yield a higher return than
comparable straight bonds, and are less risky than the stock
into which they can be converted. In view of their hybrid
character, convertible bonds are more difficult to understand
than straight bonds or stocks. That is why they are less
suitable as an investment vehicle for the small, inexperienced
investor than for the professional, well-educated portfolio
manager. In order to make successful investments in convertible bonds, investors should not only be able to correctly
predict future movements of the main determinants underlying their values, but they should also be able to determine the
degree to which these values are affected by such movements.
The impact of these movements on bond values will generally
be different in magnitude for different convertible bonds. It
is therefore of critical importance to determine this
magnitude for all convertible bonds under consideration
before making any selection for investment purposes. Indeed,

in order to make such a selection in a meaningful way, one needs to know *in advance* in what direction and to what degree values of different convertible bonds are affected by any set of expected changes in underlying determinants. We will show in the following chapters what the crucial determinants are, and explain in detail how changes in different convertible bond values can be figured out on the basis of given expectations about the future course of these determinants.

In view of the complexity of the calculations involved, small unsophisticated investors are probably better off with buying shares of mutual funds that specialize in convertible bonds than with directly investing their money in the convertibles themselves. This way, they can also benefit from the diversification and the professional management services offered by these funds. Nowadays, investors can choose among more convertible bond funds than ever before. In 1986, the number of such funds in the United States increased by 80 percent from 10 to 18.[1] This fast growth is likely to result in stronger competition among these funds, which in turn can be expected to create a need for a better investment performance and to lead over time to the use of more sophisticated management techniques. In most cases, convertible bonds are still managed in traditional ways, by means of relatively simple techniques based on the so-called *conversion premium*, and the *premium recovery* or *payback period*. The conversion premium is the amount paid by the investor over the value of the shares that he or she can acquire through immediate conversion of the bonds, while its recovery or payback period indicates the number of years after which the total interest earned on the bond equals the premium. While the conversion premium can very easily be determined for any given convertible bond, and while the relative magnitudes of the conversion premiums of different bonds provide some useful information in selecting them for investment purposes, it is much too simple a tool of analysis and the information that it provides is far too inadequate for coping with the complexity of these hybrid securities. The information contained in the premium recovery period is equally very limited. Although it gives some indication of the relative attractiveness of convertible bonds over their underlying stock, it completely ignores all bond interests earned after the payback period and, in its simplest version, it also ignores the time value of money.

Additional and more powerful information can be obtained by means of the more sophisticated techniques described in this text on the basis of modern stock option theory. The relevance of option theory stems from the fact that the conversion feature of a convertible bond is in fact a special kind of stock option, namely the so-called *conversion option*. This option entitles the holder of a convertible bond to convert that bond into shares of common stock of a corporation (which is almost always the issuer of the bond) according to certain terms and during a certain period of time. These terms usually specify the total face value of convertible bonds for which one share of common stock can be obtained at conversion. This total face value is generally referred to as the *conversion price*. In view of the nature of its conversion option, any convertible bond can be considered the equivalent of a straight bond with an attached option to exchange the straight bond for shares of the common stock underlying the convertible. As this conversion feature is nothing but a special kind of stock option, the option approach to convertible bonds is in fact very natural. In addition, it is also very powerful, due to the highly developed nature of modern option theory. Superior investment results can therefore be expected from decisions based on this approach.

Although convertible bonds were considered less important securities by the investment community in the past, their market expanded rapidly in more recent years. Several hundreds of them are traded on the New York Stock Exchange, other exchanges, and over the counter, and their number is steadily increasing over time. Disregarding convertible bond issues created in mergers, Salomon Brothers Inc. estimates that the annual issuance of convertible bonds in the U.S. rose 20-fold from $600 million in 1979 to $12 billion in 1985, while annual corporate issues of public straight bonds and notes in the U.S. only rose by 287 percent from $23.2 billion to $89.8 billion in the same period.[2] The share of convertibles in all public corporate debt issues correspondingly increased from an estimated 2.52 percent to 11.79 percent between 1979 and 1985. These figures underscore the growing importance of the convertible bond market relative to the corporate bond market as a whole, and suggest that both corporations and investors show increasingly more interest in convertible issues. As a result, the number of convertible bond funds can be expected to increase further in the years ahead, as a larger number of outstanding issues leaves more room for diversification and selection.

Corporations consider convertible bonds a cheap source of funds, as a convertible always has a substantially lower coupon rate than a straight bond issued by the same company at the same point in time. These coupon savings currently range from 2 to 4 percentage points for domestic issues. In compensation for that lower rate, investors receive the right to exercise the conversion option. If it were not for this conversion option, the lower coupon rate would cause the convertible to be worth less than a newly issued straight bond, forcing it to sell below par. The lower coupon rate and the conversion premium are determined in such a way that the total market value of the convertible bond at the time of issue is estimated to be close to its face value. The better the prospect for capital gains of a company's stock, the more valuable any conversion option on that stock, and therefore the lower a coupon rate and the higher a premium the company can afford on any convertible bond issue. All other things being equal, companies will be more interested in issuing convertible bonds instead of straight bonds, the higher the coupon rate on current straight bond issues, and the more attractive its stock to investors. Indeed, the higher the coupon rate on straight bond issues, the greater the need for finding cheaper sources of funds, and the more attractive its stock to investors, the lower the cost of funds raised through convertible bond issues. In addition to being attracted by lower interest costs, highly leveraged companies may also prefer to issue convertible as opposed to straight bonds as a way of building up more equity over time. There is a catch, however. If the bonds are converted into stock when the share price is much higher than at the time of issue of the bond, the company might have been better off issuing more expensive straight bonds, and redeeming them later on with the proceeds from selling new common stock at the much higher price. To avoid this kind of opportunity loss, issuers usually reserve to themselves the right to redeem convertible issues prematurely at a predetermined price if the stock price exceeds the conversion price by a certain percentage, or even unconditionally after a certain date. Convertible bonds that can be redeemed before maturity are said to be *callable*, and the predetermined price is referred to as the *call price*. This "callability" feature obviously makes them less attractive to investors. For that reason, callable convertible bonds must have a higher coupon rate than noncallable bonds, all other things being equal. While call protection of bondholders was nearly unheard of in the convertible bond market prior to late 1982, it has now become a standard provision that usually applies for a period of two years.

In view of the fact that the conversion option entitles holders of convertible bonds to acquire shares of underlying common stock at a fixed conversion price, they always benefit from a rise in the market price of that stock, whereas straight bondholders generally[3] do not benefit from such a rise at all. In exchange for this conversion privilege, investors in convertible bonds are willing to accept a lower current yield. This also means that they are willing to pay a price for the convertible that is greater than the value of its straight bond characteristics, that is, they are willing to pay a premium for the conversion privilege over what they would have paid if the bond were not convertible. The value of the straight bond characteristics of a convertible bond is usually called its *investment value*, while the premium as a fraction of this investment value is usually referred to as the *premium over investment value*. This investment value, and therefore also the total market value of a convertible bond, is sensitive to interest rate fluctuations in the same way as is the value of a straight bond. This implies that, all other things being equal, convertible bond investors benefit from falling interest rates, and incur losses when interest rates rise.[4]

The major relative advantages of a convertible bond over its underlying stock are that (1) it typically offers a higher current yield than the stock, that is, the interest yield on the bond usually exceeds the dividend yield on the stock, and (2) it decreases much less in value than the stock in case of a sharp decline in the stock price. The reason for the second advantage is that the convertible bond value cannot fall below its investment value, in view of the fact that the convertible will never lose its straight bond features, no matter how deep the decline in the stock price. In other words, the investment value can be considered a floor to the value of the bond, whereas such a floor does not exist for the stock price. Convertible bonds are in this sense less risky than their underlying stock. The investor also pays for these advantages in the form of a premium, namely the *conversion* premium that was defined earlier in this chapter as the premium that he pays over the current value of the shares of common stock that he would receive through immediate exercise of his conversion option. This latter value is referred to as the bond's *conversion value*. The premium also covers the right of the bondholder to *delay* the exercise of the conversion option until a later date, which offers him the possibility of cashing in on any future stock price increases, while still benefiting from the straight bond characteristics of his convertible bonds until he decides to convert them. Finally, it should also be mentioned that the stock underlying a convertible bond has a single relative advantage over the bond, which consists in the bigger capital gains that are realized by the stockholder when the stock price soars. This is due to the fact that convertible bonds increase less than proportionately in value than their underlying stock.

In addition to the concepts referred to in this chapter, we will also define and discuss a number of other basic concepts in the next chapter, with special attention to the different *value* concepts used in convertible bond analysis. These value concepts play an important role in Chapter 3, in which the value of convertible bonds is determined on the basis of stock option theory. First, we discuss basic principles of call option valuation, and apply them to the conversion option of a convertible bond. Next, we show how specific call option values can be derived within the well-known Black-Scholes framework, and how the Black-Scholes formula is adjusted for the purpose of determining the value of a conversion option. Finally, we illustrate the model by a comprehensive numerical example, and discuss the meaning of the traditional concepts of conversion premium and premium over investment value in the context of the option approach to convertible bond valuation.

Based on the valuation principles described in Chapter 3, we then analyze the problem of selecting convertible bonds for investment purposes in Chapter 4. In that chapter, we first derive some basic properties of the investment value, the value of the conversion option, and the value of the convertible bond as a whole. Next, it is shown in detail for a sample of hypothetical convertible bonds how expected bond returns can be derived from given expected returns on the stock market portfolio, and from given expected changes in the rates of interest. Once the expected returns have been determined for the different convertible bonds under consideration, they can be ranked in order of preference on the basis of the relative magnitudes of these returns. We conclude the chapter with a discussion of the role of risk in the selection process, and outline the application of Markowitz' portfolio model and a simpler multi-index model to convertible bond selection.

The ranking procedure of Chapter 4 is extended in Chapter 5 to include convertible Euro-bonds. The main difference between convertible Euro-bonds and convertible domestic bonds consists in the role played by foreign currencies. Whereas the value of a convertible domestic bond is independent of foreign exchange rates, they are a major determinant of the return on convertible Euro-bonds, and can be considered a third dimension of their valuation and selection in addition to the dimensions common to domestic convertibles, namely interest rates and stock prices. This third dimension substantially increases the profit potential of convertible bond investments but, at the same time, it complicates the analysis of the investment decision to a considerable degree. Convertible Euro-bonds are principally sold outside the country of the issuer. They may or may not be denominated in the same currency as their underlying common stock. If they are not, two different exchange rates are involved from the investor's point of view, namely the exchange rate between some reference currency and the currency in which the bonds are denominated, as well as the exchange rate between the currencies in which the bonds and their underlying stock are denominated. For example, if a U.S. investor buys German mark–denominated bonds that are convertible into yen–denominated stock of a Japanese corporation, her return on these bonds will be affected by the future course of the following two exchange rates: (1) the exchange rate between the U.S. dollar in the role of reference currency and the German mark and (2) the exchange rate between the German mark and the Japanese yen. The specific rule of either exchange rate is discussed in Chapter 5, followed by a number of concluding comments in Chapter 6.

One final remark is in order in this introduction. Although we focus on convertible bonds throughout this text, it should be emphasized *that the selection techniques of Chapter 4 can be applied to any combination of convertible and straight (domestic) bonds.* This can be done simply by treating any straight bond as just a special case of a convertible bond, namely a convertible bond with an *infinite* conversion price. A conversion option with an infinite conversion price is indeed worthless, as conversion can never take place at that price. A convertible bond with an infinite conversion price is therefore equivalent to a straight bond whose characteristics are identical to the straight bond characteristics of the convertible under consideration. In practice, it suffices to consider a very large conversion price that is large enough to make the value of the conversion option negligibly small. When processing the data on a computer, one could, for example, simply take the largest power of 10 that can be handled by both the hardware and the software. By extension, *it is also possible to apply the selection techniques of Chapter 5 to any combination of convertible, straight, domestic, and international bonds.* Indeed, not only can we consider a straight bond a special case of a convertible bond, but a domestic bond can also be considered a special case of a Euro-bond, namely a Euro-bond for which all relevant exchange rates are identical to 1. It can be concluded, therefore, that *the selection techniques described in this text not only apply to convertible bond management, but also to bond portfolio management in general.*

NOTES

1. See the November 1986 issue of *Money* magazine, page 174.

2. See *1985 Prospects for Financial Markets* and *Prospects for Financial Markets in 1987* by Salomon Brothers, Inc., New York.

3. The value of a straight bond can only rise in reaction to a rise in the price of the stock of the issuing company, if this rise in the stock price is accompanied by a reduction in the default risk of the bond.

4. It will be shown later in this text that the value of a bond's conversion option is sensitive to interest rate fluctuations as well, and that the investment value and the value of the conversion option always move in opposite directions in reaction to any given change in interest rates. The impact of such a change on the investment value is usually larger than its impact on the value of the conversion option. The total bond value itself will therefore typically move in the same direction as the investment value in response to interest rate fluctuations.

2

Basic Concepts

DEFINITION OF BASIC VALUE CONCEPTS

The concepts discussed in this section play a fundamental role in the process of valuing and selecting convertible bonds. They will be used again and again in the discussion of the topics ahead, and the reader is invited to study them thoroughly before proceeding to the next chapter.

Before introducing these value concepts, let us first repeat that *convertible bonds are securities that*

1. *have all the characteristics of straight bonds;*

2. *entitle the holder of these bonds to convert them into stock of the issuing company, during a certain period of time and according to certain terms specified at the time of issuance.*

This provision for conversion is nothing more than an option for the bondholder to exchange the bonds for the "underlying" stock during a certain period of time according to some *conversion ratio*(r_c). This ratio determines how many shares of common stock can be obtained per unit of nominal bond value. The *nominal bond value* (B_n) is by definition the *face* value that is printed on the bond. It is sometimes also referred to as the bond's *par value*. As opposed to the market value of the bond, it has no other meaning than to serve as a *reference value*. The unit of nominal bond value is usually $1,000, at least for convertible bonds that are denominated in U.S. dollars.

The conversion ratio may or may not be specified as such. If not, it can always be derived from a specified *conversion price* (p_c) of the underlying stock, which expresses the price per share that must be paid in terms of nominal bond value when the conversion takes place. It is easily seen that the conversion ratio simply is the reciprocal of the conversion price. For example, if the unit of nominal bond value is $1,000, a conversion price of $40 would correspond to a conversion ratio of $1,000/$40 = 25 shares for each bond of $1,000. Or, conversely, a conversion ratio of 25 corresponds to a conversion price of 1/25 of a unit of nominal bond value, that is, $1,000/25 = $40 per share. Remark that whereas the conversion ratio expresses a number of shares per unit of nominal bond value, the conversion price of the bonds is expressed in terms of monetary units per share.

As is sometimes stipulated in the conversion terms of the bond, some *side* or *margin payments* (M) may be required at the time of conversion, to be paid either by the bondholder or by the issuing company. This means that either bonds and money are exchanged for common stock, or bonds are exchanged for common stock and money. These side payments could be required either because they are explicitly stipulated in the conversion terms, or because the conversion ratio, as derived from the conversion price, may not be an integer.

In the latter case some rule is specified that determines the amount of the side payments that accounts for the fraction in the noninteger conversion ratio. Generally, three different fraction rules are being used in practice. They are described somewhat later in this chapter after the introduction of the main value concepts of convertible bonds. These are:

1. the so-called *investment value* (I) of the bond, which represents the value that the convertible bond would currently have without any conversion option, *inclusive of accrued interest*;

2. the *option value* (O) of the bond, which represents the current value of the conversion option of the bond, that is, the value the bond would currently have without any straight bond features;

3. the *bond value* (B) itself, that is, the current value of the convertible bond with all its straight bond and conversion option features, *inclusive of accrued interest*. As opposed to the above-mentioned nominal bond value B_n, the bond value represents the intrinsic value of the bond that corresponds to its market price in an efficient capital market;

4. the so-called *conversion value* (B_c) of the bond, which represents the current value of all shares of common stock that could be obtained by the bondholder in exchange for the bond by *immediate* conversion, plus the net value of any accompanying side payments received by the bondholder minus the value of any accompanying side payments paid by him.

It is important to note that each of these four different value concepts will be used either in dollar terms or as a fraction of the nominal bond value. We will denote them, as indicated above, by the capital letters I, O, B, and B_c when they are expressed in dollar terms, and by the lowercase letters i, o, b, and b_c when expressed as a fraction of the nominal value.

DETERMINING THE INVESTMENT VALUE

One way in which the investment value of a convertible bond could be determined is by observing the current price of "straight" bonds with characteristics that are similar to the nonconversion characteristics of the convertible bond. Assuming that the capital market is pricing straight bonds efficiently, one might then consider the price (inclusive of accrued interest) of such a straight bond a good approximation of the investment value of the convertible bond.

This method, however, has two major drawbacks. First, it will not always be possible to find marketable straight bonds with characteristics that are sufficiently close to those of the convertible bond under consideration. The characteristics that must match are (1) the amount of the interest payments and the principal repayment, as a fraction of the nominal value, to which the bondholder is entitled and (2) the timing of these payments.

Second, even in the unlikely event that there would be a complete match between the characteristics of a straight bond and those of the convertible bond, the two types of bonds may not belong to the same risk class. In such a case, the market price of the straight bond would not truly reflect the investment value of the convertible bond, since normally bond prices are also determined by the degree of credit risk, as reflected by the bond ratings that are regularly published by Moody's Investors Service and by Standard and Poor's. If the issuing companies of matching straight and convertible bonds have different ratings, the straight bond price would have to be adjusted for those differences.

A better method for finding the investment value of a convertible bond consists in determining the present value of all the future interest and principal payments that the bondholder would receive, if he keeps the bond until maturity. The techniques used for determining this present value are identical to those used in the valuation of straight bonds. The general idea can be expressed by the following present value formula:

$$i = \sum_{k=1}^{\tau} \frac{c}{(1 + \rho')^k} + \frac{v}{(1 + \rho')^{\tau}} . \qquad (2.1)$$

The right-hand side of this equation represents the present value of all future payments as a fraction of the nominal bond value; v is the fraction of the nominal bond value that represents the *redemption value* of the bond, which by definition is the principal repayment at the time of maturity; c is the coupon value as a fraction of the face value; τ is the number of future interest payments and, finally, ρ' stands for the discount rate per coupon period that is appropriate for the bond's risk class.[1]

As an example, let us consider a convertible bond with a nominal value of $5,000 and annual interest payments that represent 6 percent of this face value. If the bond will be redeemed exactly 7 years from now at 102 percent, then its investment value at a discount rate of 12 percent per year would be determined by the above present value formula as follows:

$$i = \sum_{k=1}^{7} \frac{6\%}{(1.12)^k} + \frac{102\%}{(1.12)^7} = 73.52\%.$$

The above formula is based on a number of simplifying assumptions. First, it assumes that the future interest and principal payments can be appropriately discounted by means of a single constant discount rate[2] that correctly reflects the bond's risk associated with its rating and its maturity. Second, this formula only expresses the investment value of a convertible bond if the remaining life of the bond contains an integer number of time intervals between consecutive interest payments. Third, it assumes zero income and capital gains tax rates. If one relaxes these assumptions, the above formula needs to be adjusted and would become much more complicated. The investment value will be discussed in more detail in Chapter 4, where Equation 2.1 will also be extended to include bonds whose maturities are not an integer number of coupon periods.

DETERMINING THE OPTION VALUE

The option value of the bond will be derived from option theory in Chapter 3 of this text. The value of the conversion option of a convertible bond will be determined in the same way in which the value of call options is determined in stock option theory. There are, however, certain differences between conversion options and regular call options that must be taken into account. They will also be explained in the next chapter.

The option value will first be determined under the assumption that the *conversion period* (the period during which the conversion option can be exercised) is expiring. This option value "at expiration," which is sometimes referred to as the *intrinsic value* of the conversion option, will be denoted by O_i. The difference between the option value (O) and this intrinsic value is referred to as the *time value* (O_t) of the conversion option, the properties of which will be extensively studied in the next chapter on the basis of the Black-Scholes option valuation model. Before this model can be applied, however, one must first determine the conversion value (B_c) of the bond, which can in turn be derived from the conversion terms stipulated on the bond and from the share price of its underlying stock.

DETERMINING THE BOND VALUE

The bond value simply is the sum of the investment value (I) and the option value (O) of the convertible bond: $B = I + O$, or, when all values are expressed as a fraction of the nominal bond value, $b = i + o$. The determination of the bond value will therefore be based on both straight bond and option valuation techniques, as discussed in detail in Chapters 3 and 4.

DETERMINING THE CONVERSION VALUE

By definition, the conversion value of a convertible bond represents the current market value of the shares of common stock into which the bond can be converted, minus (plus) any side payments paid (received) by the bondholder at the time of conversion.

Therefore if, for any given convertible bond with nominal bond value B_n, N represents the number of shares that are received at conversion, if M represents the side or margin payments paid by the bondholder (margin payments received by her being represented by a negative M-value), and if, finally, S represents the share price of the underlying stock, then the conversion value is defined as a fraction of the nominal value by the following equation:

$$b_c = \frac{NS - M}{B_n} .$$

(2.2)

As opposed to the conversion ratio, the number N of shares is always an integer. For a major part, the margin payments may be required by the conversion terms on the bond, and for only a small part they may be related to rounding procedures due to the indivisibility of common stock shares.

In order to clarify the latter point, let us assume that a conversion price (p_c) has been specified on the bond. Then the theoretical number of shares that can be obtained in exchange for the bond is by definition equal to B_n/p_c. If this ratio has an integer value, then $N = B_n/p_c$. However, if it is not an integer, then some *fraction rule* will apply, which is usually one of the following three:

a. the above ratio is rounded to the nearest greater integer, in which case some adjustments must be made in the form of side payments paid by the bondholder;

b. the above ratio is rounded to the nearest smaller integer, in which case adjustments must be made in the form of side payments received by the bondholder;

c. the fraction in the value of the above ratio is negated.

In each of these cases, N is equal to the correspondingly rounded value of the ratio B_n/p_c. On the other hand, ignoring any side payments that are unrelated to such rounding procedures, M would be zero under fraction rule (c), and determined by the following equation under rules (a) and (b):

$$M = Np_c - B_n. \qquad (2.3)$$

In order to obtain the total value for M, this outcome must then be added to any regular margin payments that may be specified in the conversion terms as part of the conversion transaction.

The rounding procedure can be illustrated by the following example. Assume that an investor wants to convert five convertible bonds of $1,000 at a conversion price of $32 per share, when the current market price for a share of common stock is $49. Under fraction rule (a) this investor would receive a number of shares that equals the nearest greater integer of $5,000/32 or 157 shares, in exchange for his five bonds and a payment of $(157)(\$32) - \$5,000 = \$24$. The conversion value would therefore be equal to $(157)(\$49) - (\$24)/\$5,000 = 1.5338$, in which case the conversion value of the bonds exceeds their nominal value by 53.38 percent.

Under fraction rule (b) this investor would receive 156 shares (which corresponds to the nearest smaller integer of $5,000/32) as well as a side payment of $\$5,000 - (156)(\$32) = \$8$, in exchange for his bonds. The conversion value of the bonds would therefore be equal to $(156)(\$49) - (-\$8)/\$5,000 = 1.5304$, which means that it would exceed their nominal value by 53.04 percent.

Finally, under fraction rule (c) the number of shares that the investor receives would be 156, as under fraction rule (b), but he would not receive any offsetting side payments. The conversion value would therefore be equal to $(156)(\$49)/\$5,000 = 1.5288$, or 152.88 percent of the nominal value of the bonds.

If a conversion ratio (r_c) is specified instead of a conversion price, one substitutes the ratio $\$1,000/r_c$ for p_c in the above ratios and formulas (assuming that the unit of nominal bond value is $\$1,000$). This means that N would be equal to the appropriately rounded value of $r_c \cdot B_n/\$1,000$, and that the margin payments related to the rounding procedure of fraction rules (a) and (b) would be determined by the following formula:

$$M = \$1,000 \, (N/r_c) - B_n.\qquad(2.4)$$

The formula for the conversion value itself would remain unchanged, as the conversion price as such does not appear herein.

From the above analysis, it should be clear that the conversion value of a convertible bond is exclusively determined by the terms of conversion and by the current market price of the underlying common stock. If the terms of conversion are fixed, any variation in the conversion value will be caused by variations in the share price of the issuing company.

NOTES

1. We use ρ' as a symbol instead of ρ to indicate that interest is compounded once per coupon period instead of continuously.

2. Theoretically, different discount rates should be considered for different future coupon periods. The use of a single discount rate therefore is implicitly based on the assumption that the applicable

discount rates for different periods are identical. If they are not, a single discount rate ρ' should be interpreted as a kind of average of the underlying different single period discount rates. A similar assumption will be made about the risk-free rate of interest r in the next chapter.

3

Valuation of Convertible Bonds

INTRODUCTION

As we mentioned before, a convertible bond is the equivalent of a straight bond with characteristics equal to the bond features of that convertible, in combination with an option to exchange that straight bond for some underlying stock. Therefore, the natural and logical approach to valuing convertible bonds consists in a straightforward application of modern option theory, which originated when Fischer Black and Myron Scholes (1973) proposed their now well-known option valuation model. Although valuation techniques for convertible bonds had been formulated in the academic literature before that date, none of them had the depth of the techniques that are available these days as a result of this important breakthrough in option theory. The first rigorous application of the Black-Scholes model to convertible bond valuation was published by Jonathan Ingersoll (1977). Whereas, today, the option approach to convertible bond valuation is widely accepted in academic circles, it still has to find its way to broad recognition and implementation in the world of professional investment practice.

As noted in the preceding chapter, the total bond value B of a convertible bond can be expressed as the sum of its investment value I and its option value O:

$$B = I + O. \tag{3.1}$$

While we also explained in that chapter how the investment value can be determined, we will concentrate in this chapter on the determination of the option value by applying the Black-Scholes valuation model to bond conversion options. To that end, we will first introduce some basic concepts, and compare bond conversion options to *regular (stock) options* that are traded on a stock option exchange, as well as to a related type of options known as (*stock purchase*) *warrants*.

A *call (put) option* entitles the holder of that option to buy (sell) a specific number of shares of a specific stock from (to) the issuer of the option at a fixed price, which is called the *exercise price* or the *striking price*. *European* options must be exercised on a specified date, while *American* options can be exercised any time *on or before* a specified date. That specified date is usually referred to as the *expiration date* of the option. As the conversion option of a convertible bond entitles the holder of that bond to acquire the underlying stock *on or before* a specified expiration date, this conversion option should be considered an American call option.

There are, however, certain differences between bond conversion options and regular call options that are worth mentioning. First of all, whereas regular call options usually have a maturity of less than a year, the conversion option of a typical convertible bond can be exercised over a period of several years. In other words, call options are short-term instruments, whereas convertible bonds are long-term instruments.

Second, the exercise price of a regular call option must be paid in cash, but any stock acquired by exercising a conversion option must be paid for with convertible bonds at their nominal or par value.

Third, conversion options are an inseparable part of convertible bonds, that cannot be detached from them and traded separately. Regular call options, on the other hand, "live a life of their own," that is, they are not issued in combination with other securities, and can be traded in an independent way at specialized option exchanges.

Fourth, conversion options can only be issued by the company whose stock served as underlying security. On the contrary, any investor can issue regular options on a given stock. This implies that issuing or exercising regular options on the stock of a company does not affect the balance sheet of that company, whereas issuing or exercising convertible bonds does, since the company itself is always directly involved as a party to such activities.[1]

Fifth, convertible bonds with specific conversion features are only issued in predetermined fixed amounts, whereas regular options can in principle be issued in unlimited amounts, since an option is created whenever two parties wish to create one.

Sixth, bond conversion options may come to an end prematurely when they are part of a *callable* convertible bond. This type of convertible can by definition be "called away" (i.e., redeemed) by the issuing company at a specified *call price* before maturity. That call price is usually several percentage points higher than the par value. Whereas most convertible bonds are callable, regular stock options never are and, in view of their relatively short life, it would be less meaningful if they were.

In many ways, bond conversion options are similar to (*stock purchase*) *warrants*. Both warrants and conversion options are call options that are issued by the firm whose stock serves as the underlying security (although occasionally the underlying stock may be that of a subsidiary or the parent company). Both may be exercised before expiration (i.e., they are American call options), but sometimes an initial waiting period is required. Also, at the time of issue both typically have a long time to expiration (e.g., ten or more years), and only fixed amounts of warrants or convertible bonds with specific characteristics are issued. Finally, issuing or exercising either type of call option will change the balance sheet of the issuing company.

Warrants and convertible bonds mainly differ in the way in which the underlying stock is acquired when the corresponding call option is exercised. Typically, a warrant, like a regular call option, is exercised by paying for the common stock in cash, while a conversion option is exercised by exchanging the convertible bonds for the acquired stock at a specified exchange rate based on the nominal bond value. As noted in the previous chapter, however, such an exchange may occasionaly be accompanied by a relatively small side payment in cash.

Warrants are often issued in combination with bonds, from which they may or may not be detachable before being exercised. Detachable warrants can be traded separately, as opposed to conversion options, which are always an inherent part of the corresponding convertibles. Sometimes the accompanying bonds may optionally be used at their par value in lieu of cash to pay the exercise price stipulated on the warrant. A convertible bondholder, on the contrary, can never use cash in lieu of the convertible bonds to pay for the stock when the conversion option is exercised. In other words, when an investor exercises a warrant, he is always allowed to keep the bond to which it was attached. But convertible bonds must always be turned in when their conversion option is exercised.

As a consequence, the impact of exercising the respective call options on the company's balance sheet will be different.

Exercise of a warrant typically leaves the company with more cash and more stock outstanding, without affecting its bond liabilities. Exercise of a conversion option, on the other hand, typically leaves the company with more stock and less (convertible) bonds, without affecting its cash position.

As both conversion options and stock purchase warrants are special cases of a call option, their value can be determined in a similar way as regular call options. That is why we will first explain valuation techniques for regular call options in the next section, before applying them to convertible bonds in the last section.

REGULAR CALL OPTION VALUATION

Introductory remarks

In this section, we will explain the basic principles of regular call option valuation, and discuss the Black-Scholes formula in detail. We first present the general properties of the *per share* value of regular call options as a function of the current share price of their underlying stock. The reason why we concentrate on the per share value of an option is that option prices are always quoted on a per share basis, even though an option contract usually covers 100 shares. In addition to the current share price, the per share value of a regular call option also depends on a number of other objective factors—namely its exercise price, its time to expiration, and the risk-free rate of interest—as well as on the investors' subjective expectations with respect to the future behavior of the stock price.

The exercise price is the contractual share price at which a fixed amount of shares (usually 100) of the underlying stock can be purchased by the option holder when exercising the option. Usually this exercise price is a multiple of $5 or $10. When established, option contracts expire about nine months later. The risk-free rate of interest is commonly considered to be the yield on Treasury bills that have roughly the same expiration date as the option.

We begin our discussion of call option valuation by concentrating on the role of the current share price (S), the exercise price (E), and the remaining time to expiration (t). For the time being, therefore, we will express the call option value per share (V_o) as a function f of these three determinants only, as shown in Equation 3.2:

$$V_o = f(S, E, t). \tag{3.2}$$

S and t are the only two arguments of this function that vary over the life of the option, as E is usally an invariable option feature that is fixed at the time of issue. In our analysis of the above value function, we will first focus on the way in which the option value depends on the current stock price level, assuming a given time to maturity. Next, we will also concentrate on how the value of an option changes when its remaining life shrinks as time goes on.

From the outset, it is useful to point out that, other things being equal, *the option value per share would be halved if both the current share price and the exercise price are halved.* This can be shown as follows. Suppose an investor has a number of options to buy 100 shares of a particular common stock at an exercise price E before a certain expiration date, and suppose a 2-for-1 stock split would occur. All other things being equal, such a stock split would cut the share price in half. Unless there are contractual provisions to adjust the terms for exercising the options in such a case, this share price reduction would deteriorate the position of the investor, as she could probably no longer exercise her options at a price that is attractive relative to the new share price. The value of the options could, however, be "immunized" against such a stock split by a contractual provision for (1) cutting the exercise price in half and (2) doubling the number of shares the investor is entitled to buy. As a result, the investor would be able to acquire the same fraction of all outstanding stock for the same total dollar investment as before the stock split. In addition, since the value of the company has not been changed by the stock split, the acquired shares of common stock still have the same value.

To illustrate this point, assume that the stock is priced at $50 a share, and that the exercise price of the option is $45. If the total number of outstanding shares is 1,000,000, and if the investor under consideration has 80 call options, she would be entitled to buy $(80)(100) = 8,000$ shares, or 0.80 percent of all shares outstanding, at a total price of $(8,000)(\$45) = \$360,000$, which represents 0.72 percent of the current company value of $(1,000,000)(\$50) = \$50,000,000$. If a 2-for-1 stock split would occur, the share price would drop to $25. Without any adjustments, the 80 options would become worthless as the investor would better buy 8,000 shares at $25 a share, than exercise her 80 options at a price of $45 a share. However, if the occurrence of the stock split would allow her to buy double the original number of shares at half the original exercise price, she could buy $(2)(80)(100)$ $= 16,000$ shares at a price of $\$45/2 = \$22.5$ per share. As before, she pays only $(16,000)(\$22.5) = \$360,000$, or 0.72 percent of the current company value of $(2,000,000)(\$25) =$ $\$50,000,000$, to acquire $16,000/2,000,000 = 0.80$ percent of all shares outstanding. Under those circumstances, there is no reason why, other things equal, the value of her options would have changed in reaction to the stock split. But since the number of shares that the option holder is entitled to buy has doubled (16,000 instead of 8,000 originally), the option value *per share* would actually be cut in half.

Summing up, this example clearly shows that, other things being equal, the option value per share is halved whenever both the exercise price and the share price are halved. This property of the value of regular call options can be expressed as follows in terms of the value function defined in Equation 3.2: $f(S, E, t)/2 = f(S/2, E/2, t)$. The left side of this equation corresponds to half the original value (per share) of an option to buy shares at an exercise price E when the current share price is S, while the right side equals the value (per share) of an option to buy the same stock at half the original exercise price when the share price is halved as well.

By extension, it is easily seen that the following more general property also applies:

$$f(S, E, t)/\lambda = f(S/\lambda, E/\lambda, t), \tag{3.3}$$

where λ represents any positive real number. If we substitute E as a value for λ in Equation 3.3, we obtain: $f(S, E, t)/E = f(S/E, E/E, t)$. In view of Equation 3.2, this formula can be reduced to: $V_o/E = f(S/E, 1, t)$. Finally, if we express the right-hand side of this equation as a value function f' of only two variables S/E and t, we obtain:

$$V_o/E = f'(S/E, t). \tag{3.4}$$

From this equation it is clear that *we can omit the exercise price of a call option as a separate determinant of the option value per share, as long as we express both the option value and the stock price as a fraction of the exercise price indicated on the option.* If we denote these fractions by V_o' and S', respectively, that is, if by definition:

$$V_o' = V_o/E \text{ and } S' = S/E, \tag{3.5}$$

Equation 3.4 can also be written as:

$$V_o' = f'(S', t).$$ \hfill (3.6)

The value of a call option at expiration

Let us now determine the per share value of a regular call option *at expiration*; that is, let us try to specify $f(S, E, 0)$ for any given value of S and E. At the time of expiration, the option holder can do one of the following: either he can let the option expire, in which case it becomes worthless, or he can exercise the option. By exercising the option, he would buy shares at a discount or at a premium relative to the current share price, depending on whether the latter is greater than or smaller than the exercise price. If the current share price is greater (smaller) than the exercise price, the option is said to be *in the money* (*out of the money*), while it is said to be *at the money* if the current share price coincides with the exercise price. Obviously, the option holder would only choose to exercise the option if he can buy the shares at a discount (i.e, if the option is in the money). In this case its value per share is equal to the difference between the current share price S and the exercise price E. Indeed, in such a case he could actually realize that same value as a profit per share, by buying the shares at the exercise price E and selling them immediately at the supposedly greater share price S. However, if the option is out of the money at expiration, this procedure would lead to a loss and it would therefore be better to let the option expire without exercise.

The above conclusions can be summarized as follows:

$$f(S, E, 0) = \max [0, (S - E)].$$ \hfill (3.7)

Indeed, according to this formula, the option value per share at expiration is equal to $(S - E)$ if $S > E$ (in the money), and to 0 if $S < E$ (out of the money).

The value function $f(S, E, 0)$, as determined by Equation 3.7, not only represents the value per share of an expiring option, but also the *intrinsic value* or *parity value* per share of a nonexpiring option. In addition, $f(S, E, t) - f(S, E, 0)$, the difference between the full option value per share and the intrinsic value per share, is usually referred to as the option's *time value* per share.

To illustrate the above formula, consider an expiring option with an exercise price of \$30. If the current share price of the underlying stock is \$39, this option would be in the money, and therefore its value per share would be equal to \$39 − \$30 = \$9. However, if the current share price is \$27, the option would be out of the money, and therefore it would have a zero value. If the option were currently not expiring, these respective values of \$9 and \$0 could still be interpreted as the option's intrinsic value per share.

Equation 3.7 is graphically illustrated in Figure 3.1. The straight line with a slope of 45° that cuts the horizontal axis at E represents the difference between the share price S and the exercise price E, which corresponds to the profit per share earned when the option is exercised. As a negative profit or loss can always be avoided by letting the option expire without exercising it, this difference only represents the option value per share if $S > E$, that is, only the solid part of the 45° line is relevant. If $S < E$ at expiration, the option's value per share is reduced to zero, and is therefore represented by a straight line that coincides with the horizontal axis. As a result, the option value per share at expiration for all possible stock prices is represented in Figure 3.1 by the kinked straight line *OEF*.

Alternatively, if we express the share price as a fraction of the exercise price, the option value per share can also be

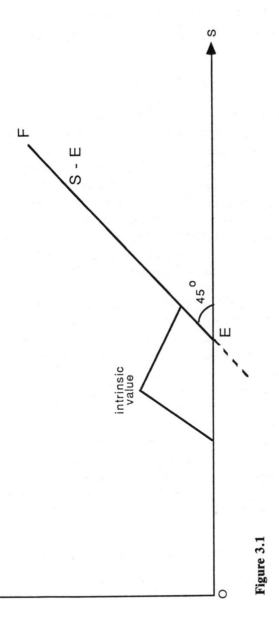

Figure 3.1

derived as a fraction of the exercise price from the following valuation formula: $f'(S/E, 0) = \max[0, (S/E) - 1]$, or, equivalently,

$$f'(S', 0) = \max(0, S' - 1). \tag{3.8}$$

For example, let us reconsider the preceding numerical example of an expiring option with an exercise price of $30. If the current share price is $39, a share of common stock would be worth 1.3 times the exercise price, and the option value per share would therefore be equal to $1.3 - 1 = 30$ percent of the exercise price. At a current price of $27, however, a share would be valued at only 90 percent of the exercise price. As this fraction is smaller than 1, the corresponding option value per share would be zero. If the option were not currently expiring, it would have an intrinsic value of 30 percent and 0 percent of the exercise price, respectively.

Equation 3.8 can also be represented by a kinked straight line, as shown in Figure 3.2, where the option value per share, as a fraction of the exercise price, corresponds to the broken line $OE'F'$.

In this subsection, we only considered regular call options at their maturity. At maturity, the option holder can only choose between exercising the option and letting it expire. This choice was completely determined by the current share price relative to the exercise price. If we consider options before their expiration date, however, we must take into account some additional factors, like the time value of money as measured by the risk-free rate of interest, and the investors' expectations about the unknown future share prices up to the time of expiration. The role of these other factors will be discussed in the next subsection.

Lower limits on the value of a call option before expiration

When considering a call option some time before expiration,

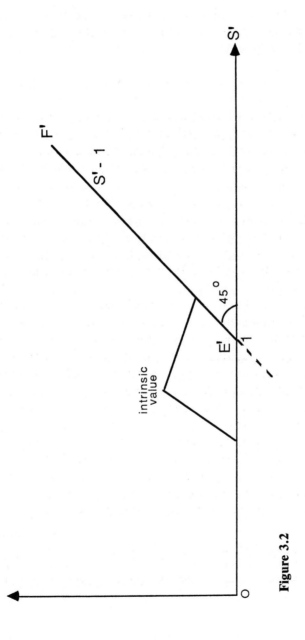

Figure 3.2

we must be careful to consider the value of all the relevant parameters *at the same point in time*. Indeed, as long as we assume money to have a positive time value, we cannot simply add or subtract monetary values of cash flows at different points in time. As is explained in elementary textbooks in finance, only the equivalents of these cash flows at one and the same point in time can be compared.

In order to determine the current option value per share, we should therefore compare the current share price to the present value of the exercise price, rather than to the exercise price itself. Indeed, if an option is exercised at some future time, the exercise price also refers to a future cash flow resulting from a future stock purchase transaction. For example, if we assume that the option is exercised at expiration, the present value of the corresponding cash flow would be equal to $E(1 + r)^{-t} = E/(1 + r)^t$, where t represents the remaining time to expiration and r the applicable risk-free rate of interest. At least this would be its present value if interest is compounded once per unit of time. In the case of continuous compounding, the financial textbooks tell us that the present value would be equal to $E \cdot e^{-rt} = E/e^{rt}$. In general, we will denote this present value of the exercise price at expiration by $PV(E, r, t)$. As this present value is proportional to E, it is also equal to E times $PV(1, r, t)$, where $PV(1, r, t)$ represents the present value of a cash flow of 1 dollar at expiration for a rate of interest $r \cdot PV(1, r, t)$ is often referred to as the *present value interest factor* at rate r for t time units. For example, the present value interest factor at 1 percent per month for 5 months would be equal to $(1 + r)^{-t} = (1.01)^{-5} = 95.15$ percent if interest is compounded on a monthly basis, and it turns out to be equal to $e^{-rt} = e^{-.05} = 95.12$ percent if interest is compounded continuously.

If $S > PV(E, r, t)$, the option holder could always realize a risk-free profit with a present value equal to $S - PV(E, r, t)$

per share, by selling the stock (possibly short, if he has no long position in it) at the current price S and buying it back at a price E by exercising the option at its expiration. If $S < PE(E, r, t)$, such an operation would lead to a loss, which could, however, always be avoided by simply letting the option expire instead. This means that the option holder can always (1) avoid losing money and (2) realize a guaranteed minimum profit per share equal to $S - PV(E, r, t)$ whenever the current stock price is high enough to make this latter expression positive. The option value per share, therefore, can never be smaller than (1) zero and (2) $S - PV(E, r, t)$:

$$V_o \geq \max[0, S - PV(E, r, t)]. \qquad (3.9)$$

For example, if interest is compounded once a month at a risk-free monthly rate of 1 percent, and if the current price of a share of common stock is \$39, the value per share of an option to buy shares at an exercise price of \$30 within the next 5 months is not smaller than \$39 $-$ (95.15 percent)(\$30) = \$10.46. As we determined before, that the given share price of \$39 implies an intrinsic value of \$9, this also means that at 5 months to expiration the option's time value is not less than \$10.46 $-$ \$9 = \$1.46 per share.

The lower limit on the option value per share described by Inequality 3.9 will be referred to as the option's *floor value*. It is represented in Figure 3.3 by the kinked line *OGH*, while the intrinsic value per share is represented by *OEF*. Point *G* on the horizontal axis corresponds to the present value of the exercise price. Therefore, the floor *OGH* is obtained by shifting the intrinsic value line *OEF* in a parallel way to the left over a distance equal to the difference between the exercise price and its present or discounted value.

Alternatively, if we express the option value per share and the share price as a fraction of the exercise price, its lower boundary is described by the following inequality:

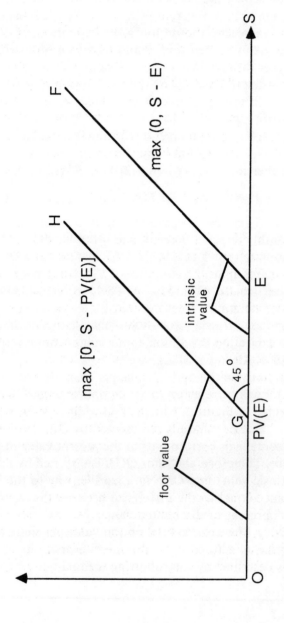

Figure 3.3

$$V_o' \geq \max[0, S' - PV(1, r, t)]. \qquad (3.10)$$

In the preceding example, we came up with a floor of \$10.46 for the option value per share 5 months to expiration. Using Inequality 3.10 instead of 3.9 would lead to a floor equal to \$10.46/\$30 = 34.87 percent of the exercise price. As we determined before, that the intrinsic value per share of this option equals 30 percent of the exercise price, its time value per share 5 months to expiration is at least 34.87 percent − 30 percent = 4.87 percent of the exercise price.

Exercising an American call option before its expiration date

From Figure 3.3 it is clear that, if at some time before maturity the stock price exceeds the discounted value of the exercise price, the option value is always strictly greater than its intrinsic value. In particular, the value of any unexpired in-the-money call option always exceeds its intrinsic value. As the intrinsic value of such an option is the profit that can be realized by exercising it and selling the acquired stock immediately thereafter, it would be more profitable to sell that option than to exercise it.

On the other hand, if an option is out of the money, its exercise price is by definition higher than the current stock price, and therefore it would be cheaper to buy the stock directly than to buy it by exercising the option. Consequently, exercising such an option would not pay at all.

Summing up, *an American call option, whether in the money or out of the money, should never be exercised before maturity*![2] This result may seem paradoxical, but can easily be explained by the fact that, when exercising a call option, only the intrinsic value of that option is realized, but not its time value. This time value can only be realized by selling the option. Therefore, the basic dilemma that any holder of an unexpired option is facing is not whether or not to exercise the option, but rather, *whether or not to sell* the option, where the alternative to selling is to let it mature. Furthermore, since American call options are never exercised before maturity, they give the option holder no real advantage over European call options. Consequently, *the value of American call options must be identical to the value of corresponding European call options with the same characteristics.* For that reason, we will no longer make a distinction between American and European call options, except where explicitly mentioned.

Additional properties of the value of a call option before expiration

Whenever an option holder can realize a profit by selling stock at the present time at its current market price S and buying it back later at the exercise price E, the present value of that profit was shown previously in this chapter ("Lower Limits on the Value of a Call Option before Expiration") to correspond to the option's floor value. When these transactions do not lead to a profit, that floor value turns out to be zero.

Let us now investigate how much the current market value of the option exceeds its floor value. We will do so at the same point in time for different stock price levels that cover a whole range, from very low to very high values of S. First, consider the case in which S is so small relative to the option's exercise price E, that it is very unlikely that it will become greater than E before the option's expiration date. As it is virtually certain that such an option will remain out of the money until that date, it is said to be *far out of the money*. In view of its very small profit potential, its market value will not significantly differ from zero; that is, it will not significantly differ from its floor value.

If, starting from such a low stock price level, we consider gradually higher levels of S, the option value would leave its floor and gradually increase, even though the floor value itself would remain zero as long as $S < PV(E, r, t)$. The reason is that even though the option cannot be profitably exercised under those circumstances, there is always a probability that the stock price may climb higher later on, and exceed $PV(E, r, t)$ sometime before the option's expiration date. If and when this happens, a profit can be realized by selling the stock and exercising the option at maturity. This prospect of future gain opportunities, in combination with the fact that one can always avoid losses by letting the option expire, causes the option to have a positive value as long as it is not too far out of the money. The better the prospect of future gains is considered to be by investors, the greater this option value. In particular, as this prospect is better the smaller the difference between the stock price and the discounted exercise price $PV(E, r, t)$, the option value will increase with increasing stock price levels. And since the floor value is constantly equal to zero in the range of stock price levels below $PV(E, r, t)$, the option's excess value over its floor value will increase in that range as well.

Let us now try to determine what happens to that excess value when we consider further increases in the stock price level beyond the discounted value $PV(E, r, t)$ of the exercise price. Beyond that level, risk-free profits could be realized by immediately selling stock at its current market price and repurchasing the stock by exercising the option at expiration. These profits are greater the higher the stock price, which causes the option's floor value to rise when higher stock prices are considered.

At the same time, however, the prospect of making even bigger profits by delaying the stock sale starts deteriorating.

In fact, in case of a decline in the stock price, such a delay would lead to smaller rather than bigger profits. Even worse, if that decline causes the stock price to become smaller than the discounted value of the exercise price, selling the stock would no longer be profitable. Obviously, the greater the current price, the greater the potential decrease in profits, and therefore the less attractive the prospect resulting from a delay in the stock sale.

This phenomenon forces the option's excess value over its floor value to gradually diminish when increasingly higher current stock prices are considered beyond the discounted exercise price. For current stock prices that are very high relative to its exercise price, that excess value will virtually have vanished and the option is said to be *deep in the money*. Its value can, for all practical purposes, be considered to coincide with its floor value. In fact, at this point the option starts behaving in the same way as the underlying stock—any change in the stock price is reflected in a matching change in the per share value of the option.

These results are graphically illustrated in Figure 3.4, where the curvilinear line V_o represents the option's market value per share. As in the preceding figures, the option's floor and intrinsic values per share are again represented by broken straight lines, that partially coincide with the horizontal axis. As was shown by Merton (1973), the curve representing the option's market value always has the convex shape shown in the figure. It can easily be verified that the excess value per share will increase with rising stock prices below the discounted exercise price $PV(E, r, t)$, but decrease with rising stock prices above that level. The maximum excess value therefore is reached when $S = PV(E, r, t)$.

Figure 3.4 also shows that the intrinsic and floor values of an option coincide at the zero level for stock prices below the discounted exercise price $PV(E, r, t)$. As a consequence, the

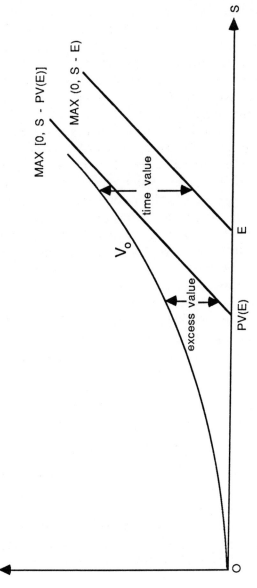

Figure 3.4

total value of the option, the excess value over its floor value, and its time value all coincide for these stock price levels.

However, if the stock price is greater than the discounted exercise price, things are more complicated. In this case the floor value is strictly greater than the intrinsic value, due to the time value of money by which the exercise price is discounted.

Furthermore, this difference between the floor and intrinsic values must be added to the option's excess value to obtain its time value. The time value therefore has two distinct components: (1) the time value of money by which the exercise price is discounted, that is, the interest that can be earned by delaying the exercise of the option until its expiration date and (2) the value derived from the prospect of possible sizable increases in realizable profits between now and the expiration date, in combination with only limited risks of profit decreases. Realizable profits go up or down together with the stock price. However, while they can increase over time in an unrestricted way, they can never turn into losses in view of the built-in zero-level floor, no matter how far the stock price would fall. Still, for deep-in-the-money options, the potential profit decreases and related risks are so great that they totally offset the chances for further gains. At this point the second component of the option's time value vanishes, so that the total option value is reduced to its floor value.

The Black-Scholes option valuation model

So far we have only determined the general shape of the curve that describes the relationship between the option value and the stock price. Thus at this point we still do not know how to determine the specific numerical value of a call option.

Black and Scholes (1973) demonstrated how this can be done under certain simplifying assumptions.[3] Their formula has gained wide recognition, and it is generally used by professional investors to estimate the value of options. Although the formula itself is not simple in its appearance, it can easily be applied, even by less experienced investors. Nowadays it is a common feature of investment packages for personal computers and it is also available to users of some of the more advanced programmable hand calculators. It specifies the option value per share V_o as follows:

$$V_o = S\Phi(d_1) - PV(E, r, t)\Phi(d_2) \qquad (3.11)$$

where

$$d_1 = \frac{\ln(S/E) + (r + .5\sigma^2)t}{\sigma\sqrt{t}}, \qquad (3.12)$$

$$d_2 = \frac{\ln(S/E) + (r - .5\sigma^2)t}{\sigma\sqrt{t}}. \qquad (3.13)$$

The symbol Φ in Equation 3.11 represents the cumulative standardized normal probability distribution. That is, $\Phi(d_1)$ and $\Phi(d_2)$ are the probabilities that a normally distributed random variable, with a mean of 0 and a standard deviation of 1, does not take values greater than d_1 and d_2, respectively. Appendix B at the end of this chapter contains a table of probabilities $\Phi(x)$ for selected values of x. $\Phi(x)$ is, in fact, an integral function of x, the values of which can be determined with a high degree of accuracy by a polynomial approximation of that function.[4]

The parameter r in the above formulas again represents the *continuously compounded* risk-free rate of interest, which implies that $PV(E, r, t) = Ee^{-rt}$ in Equation 3.11. Finally, the symbol σ^2, which appears in Equations 3.12 and 3.13, stands for the *volatility* of the stock price as measured by the *variance per unit of time* of the *continuously compounded* rate of return on the stock.[5] It should be noted that the variance, and not its square root (the standard deviation) is proportional to the length of the time period over which it is defined. In other words, if one chooses to reduce the unit of time from 1 year to 1 month, then the volatility is reduced to 1/12 or 8.33 percent of its original magnitude. The standard deviation, however, would be reduced to $1/\sqrt{12}$ or 28.78 percent of its original size. Therefore, *when redefining the time unit, one should first adjust the variance in the same proportion, then take the square root to determine the adjusted value of the standard deviation.* First adjusting the standard deviation, and then raising the adjusted standard deviation to the power 2 to determine the variance, would definitely lead to incorrect volatility figures. For example, first adjusting the standard deviation in the above example would reduce σ to 8.33 percent (instead of 28.78 percent) of its original value and, consequently, the volatility σ^2 would be reduced to $1/(12)^2$ or 1/144 (instead of 1/12) of its original value.

In total, the Black-Scholes model has five parameters, namely $S, E, r, t,$ and σ^2. With the exception of the volatility, they all can be directly observed. The volatility cannot be observed, as it reflects investors' expectations about the future behavior of the rate of return on the stock. It can, however, be estimated from historical stock price fluctuations. Cash dividend payments do not show up as a parameter because, strictly speaking, the formula only applies if no cash dividends are paid during the remaining life of the option.

To illustrate the formula, let us reconsider the example from the previous section, in which we assumed a risk-free rate of interest of 1 percent per month, a current stock price of $39, a remaining life of 5 months, and an exercise price of $30. Using the symbols of this chapter, this means that $r = 1$

percent per month, that $t = 5$ months, that $S = \$39$, and that $E = \$30$. In addition, let us assume that the stock's volatility σ^2 equals $(28\text{ percent})^2 = .0784$ per year, or $.0784/12 = .0065$ per month. The values of parameters d_1 and d_2 in the Black-Scholes formula can then be determined as follows:

$$d_1 = \frac{\ln(39/30) + 5[.01 + (.5)(.0065)]}{\sqrt{(.0065)(5)}} = 1.8228$$

$$d_2 = \frac{\ln(39/30) + 5[.01 - (.5)(.0065)]}{\sqrt{(.0065)(5)}} = 1.6425$$

Next, we can derive the following approximate values for $\Phi(d_1)$ and $\Phi(d_2)$ from the table of Appendix B at the end of this chapter:

$$\Phi(d_1) = \Phi(1.8228) = .9641$$

$$\Phi(d_2) = \Phi(1.6425) = .9505$$

By using a suitable computer program, more accurate values of .9656 for $\Phi(d_1)$ and .9495 for $\Phi(d_2)$ can be found, which lead to the following option value per share:

$$V_o = S\Phi(d_1) - Ee^{-rt}\Phi(d_2)$$
$$= (\$39)(.9656) - (\$30)(e^{-.05})(.9495)$$
$$= \$10.56$$

Apparently, the value of this option is only slightly higher than its previously determined floor value of \$10.46. Since we determined before that this option has an intrinsic value of \$9, we must also conclude that its time value per share is $\$10.56 - \$9 = \$1.56$. This time value consists for $\$30(1 - e^{-.05}) = \$1.46$ of the time value of money by which the exercise price is discounted, and for the $0.10 excess value that reflects the degree by which the chances of making even higher profits from a further increase in the stock price outweigh the risk of a limited decline in profits that would result from a decrease in the stock price.

Some important conclusions can be drawn about the direction in which changes in the parameter values affect the option value. It can be shown that *a call option is more valuable*:

1. *the higher the current stock price relative to the exercise price,*
2. *the higher the risk-free rate of interest,*
3. *the longer the remaining time to expiration, and*
4. *the greater the volatility of the underlying stock.*

Finally, by dividing both sides of Equation 3.11 by the exercise price E, we obtain:

$$V_o/E = (S/E)\ \Phi(d_1) - PV(1, r, t)\ \Phi(d_2), \tag{3.14}$$

$$= (S/E)\ \Phi(d_1) - e^{-rt}\ \Phi(d_2). \tag{3.15}$$

These equations confirm that the exercise price as such is irrelevant in the determination of the option's value, as long as both the option value per share and the current stock price are expressed as a fraction of the given exercise price. Indeed, the right-hand sides of Equations 3.12, 3.13, and 3.14 or 3.15 only depend on the ratio S/E, and not on the prices S and E as such. Thus the current stock price in the above example was equal to 39/30 or 130 percent of the option's exercise price, and its corresponding value per share turned out to be equal to 10.56/30 or 35.2 percent of its exercise price.

Impact of dividend payments on the value of a call option

Strictly speaking, the Black-Scholes formula discussed above only applies to European call options. Therefore, it can only be used for valuing American call options if early excercise is most unlikely. Such is not the case, however, when the underlying stock is expected to pay dividends during the life of the American call option. The reason is that the option holder is not compensated for any dilution of the stock's value due to cash dividend payments. As a consequence, early exercise of the option may pay if a large enough dividend payment is expected soon enough. The conclusion, therefore, is that *the Black-Scholes value of an American call option on a dividend-paying stock is at best only an approximation of its true value.* Fortunately, the Black-Scholes formula can be generalized to include the case of American call options on dividend-paying stocks. The extended model was originally developed by Richard Roll (1977), later simplified by Geske (1979), and finally perfected by Whaley (1981). As a detailed analysis of the implications of dividend payments on convertible bond valuation is beyond the scope of this text, we will not discuss this extended model in an explicit way. Interested readers are referred to the above publications for more information on this subject. A brief description of the generalized formula itself can be found in Haugen (1986).

This second section covered the basic principles of call option valuation, inclusive of the Black-Scholes formula, with a short discussion of the implications of dividend payments. These principles will be applied to the conversion option of a convertible bond in the next section. Once the value O of that conversion option is determined, it suffices to add it to the investment value I to obtain the value B of the bond as a whole.

VALUATION OF CONVERTIBLE BONDS

Cases in which early conversion is possible

As the conversion option is an American option, we must

consider the possibility that it is exercised before maturity on a *voluntary* basis. Such an early voluntary conversion may only be profitable in a limited number of cases, namely:

1. the case in which the underlying stock is expected to pay dividends during the life of the conversion option;
2. the case in which the conversion terms change over time in favor of the issuing company;
3. the case in which side payments occur at the time of conversion.

While the first case is represented by virtually all existing issues in the convertible bond market, the latter cases are only represented by a small minority of them. Dividend payments can be taken into account by applying the extended option valuation model (referred to above) to the conversion option of convertible bonds. In view of the complexity of that model, however, the case of early conversion due to dividend payments will not be analyzed in this text. *This extended model is also much less relevant to convertible bond valuation than to regular American call option valuation.* Indeed, dividend payments will normally not induce any premature voluntary conversion, *as long as their benefit is not considered greater than the benefit of the interest payments on the bond.* By converting the bonds into stock, the bondholder will receive a stream of dividend payments but, at the same time, he foregoes the opportunity to receive a stream of interest payments. If interest and dividend dates coincide, the benefit of the interest payments will be greater than the benefit of the dividend payments, *if the current interest yield on the bond is greater than the current dividend yield on the stock.* As this is usually the case, *dividend payments will generally not induce early conversion of the bond.*

The above reasoning has to be adjusted somewhat if the dividend date and the bond coupon date do not coincide. In practice, dividends are generally paid quarterly, while interest on the bond is usually paid on a semiannual basis. In other words, dividend and interest payments will, in general, occur at different times and with different frequencies. Under those circumstances, any comparison between the dividend and interest streams should not only be based on the relative size of these payments, but also on their timing. This not only means that the time value of money must be taken into account. In view of the fact that the bondholder does not receive any accrued interest at conversion, it also means that the conversion decision will generally depend on the exact timing of the conversion relative to both the dividend date and the coupon date. For example, all other things being equal, it is obvious that a conversion right after an interest date and just before a dividend date is more profitable than a conversion just before an interest date and right after a dividend date. Still, *as long as the difference between the current interest yield on the bond and the current dividend yield on the stock is large enough, early conversion is not going to be sufficiently profitable to make its occurrence likely.*

In the second case, in which the conversion terms change in favor of the issuing company, such a premature conversion is, on the contrary, not unlikely. As a result, the possibility of early conversion cannot as easily be ignored in this case as in the first case. As a discussion of the valuation of bonds with changing conversion terms is beyond the scope of this analysis, we refer to Ingersoll (1977) for more details.

In the third case, in which side payments are required at conversion, early conversion is again most unlikely. Side payments will never induce such an early conversion if they are received by the issuing company, or if they are relatively small and received by the bondholder. As, in practice, the bondholder will only receive side payments in application of certain fraction rules, they are in fact always very small. A detailed analysis of the impact of side payments on the early conversion decision is presented in Appendix A at the end of this chapter. As the possibility of a premature conversion in this third case can be ruled out for all practical purposes, side payments will explicitly be taken into account throughout the rest of this text.

It should be noted that the bondholder may also be *forced* by the issuing company to exercise his conversion option prematurely, at least if he is the holder of callable convertible bonds. These are convertible bonds that can be "called away" by the issuing company, which means that the company has the right (option) to redeem the bonds at a predetermined call price before maturity. This right may be conditional or unconditional. If and when the company decides to exercise this right, the bondholder has a choice between only two alternatives: either he accepts the call price at which his bonds are redeemed, or he exercises the conversion option. This means that he is practically forced to convert his bonds if the second alternative is more attractive to him than the first. As the issuing company will typically exercise its call option when the conversion value of the bonds exceeds the call price by a substantial amount, the bondholder will generally respond by exercising the conversion option.

It should be noted that most convertible bonds are callable, and that their callability is a most important drawback from the investor's point of view. As the value of a callable convertible bond is not likely to rise significantly above the call price, it may be substantially less than the value of a comparable noncallable bond. Since the likelihood of early conversion of callable convertibles is relatively high, it should be taken into account when determining their value. It is worthwhile to mention that the impact of the callability feature on the value of a convertible bond has thoroughly been analyzed for convertible zero-coupon bonds and convertible consol bonds. However, since these bonds are rare or nonexistent they have virtually no practical meaning. The truth is that the valuation of callable, coupon-bearing, convertible bonds with finite maturity is extremely difficult, and that no simple formula is available. For the sake of simplicity, we will therefore ignore any callability feature in the present text. More information on the valuation of callable convertible bonds, with a discussion of relevant numerical procedures, can be found in Brennan and Schwartz (1977).

Basic principles of convertible bond valuation when early conversion is excluded

According to the definition in Chapter 2, the investment and option values of a convertible bond represent the values of its bond and conversion features, respectively. In this connection, it is useful to think of the convertible bond as a combination of two separate and distinguishable securities, the first of which is a straight bond with characteristics identical to the bond features of the convertible bond, and the second of which is an option to convert the first security into shares of the underlying stock with conversion terms identical to those stipulated on the convertible bond. The values of these imaginary securities would then correspond to the investment value I and the option value O, respectively, while their sum would equal the bond value B in conformity with Equation 3.1.

As the second imaginary security has the same conversion terms as the convertible bond, it entitles its holder to exchange the first imaginary security for the same number N of shares into which the convertible bond can be converted. By exercising this option, he foregoes the opportunity of receiving principal and interest payments associated with the first security. Ingersoll (1977) proved that if no dividends are paid to stockholders, if no margin payments are required at conversion, if the conversion terms are constant over time, and if conditions of perfect competition prevail in the capital markets, *the conversion option will never be exercised prior to maturity or call.* This result was based on a similar property derived by Merton (1973) for call options and stock purchase warrants. It is clear that, as long as we can exclude the possibility of early exercise, *the conversion option represented by the second imaginary security must have the same value as a stock purchase warrant with identical maturity, that entitles the warrant holder to buy the same number of shares for which the convertible bond can be exchanged, at a total cost equal to the value of the first imaginary security at the time of maturity of the conversion option.* Indeed, exchanging the first imaginary security for the shares at maturity is equivalent to buying them at a price equal to its value at maturity.

As we pointed out in the beginning of this section, the value of the first imaginary security is nothing but the investment value I of the convertible bond, which represents the present value of all future interest and principal payments to which the bondholder is entitled. If I_m denotes this investment value at the time of maturity of the conversion option, the total cost of exercising the warrant defined in the above emphasized statement is then equal to I_m. Since the warrant is used to buy the same number N of shares for which the convertible bond can be exchanged, the corresponding exercise price of the warrant is equal to I_m/N. As warrants are valued the same way as call options, this implies that the value per share of the warrant or, in other words, the option value per share of the convertible bond is equal to $f(S, I_m/N, t)$, where f is the value function discussed above ("Regular Call Option Valuation") and t the time to maturity of the conversion option.

The conversion may be accompanied by a margin payment. If positive, this payment is to be made by the bondholder or, if negative, by the issuing company. In Chapter 2, we represented the amount of this margin payment by the symbol M. It can be taken into account by adding this amount to the investment value I_m, as an additional price to pay for the N shares that are received at conversion. In general, therefore, the option value per share of the convertible bond will be equal to $f[S, (I_m + M)/N, t]$. As a total of N shares are obtained at the time of conversion, the option value of the convertible bond must be equal to:

$$O = Nf[S, (I_m + M)/N, t] \qquad (3.16)$$

In view of Property 3.3 of value function f, this can be simplified to:

$$O = f(NS, I_m + M, t). \qquad (3.17)$$

As most convertible bonds mature at the same time as their conversion option, I_m will typically be equal to the bond's redemption value, which in turn coincides with its nominal value B_n in virtually all cases. If the conversion period ends before the maturity date of the bond, I_m has to be figured out by means of Equation 2.1 or a more sophisticated present-value formula, using the same rate of interest r as is used to determine the current investment value I. For the sake of simplicity, we indeed assume that interest rates are constant over time, that all future single-period interest rates are equal to the current single-period interest rate.[6]

Similar to what we did for regular call options above ("Regular Call Option Valuation"), the value per share $f(S, (I_m + M)/N, t]$ of the conversion option of a convertible bond can be decomposed into (1) its intrinsic value per share max $[0, S - (I_m + M)/N]$ and (2) its time value per share. This latter part, in turn, consists of (a) the dollar amount by which the payment of the exercise price $(I_m + M)/N$ at maturity must be discounted to obtain its present value and (b) some excess value that accounts for the possibility of increased profits at conversion due to higher stock prices later on, in combination with only limited risks for profit decreases that would result from lower stock prices. In other words, part (a) of the time value per share reflects the *certain* profit that can be realized at the current stock price S, while part (b) reflects the value of the *uncertain* excess profits that result from changes in the stock price between the present and the time of maturity. In conformity with the previous section, part (a) can also be expressed as the difference between the bond's floor value per share $\max\{0, S - PV[(I_m + M)/N]\}$ and its intrinsic value per share. The intrinsic value, the floor value, and the total current value of the bond's conversion option are represented on a per share basis in Figure 3.5. This figure is analogous to Figure 3.4, in which we represented the same value concepts for the call option.

The same value concepts can also be defined for the bond as a whole, rather than on a per share basis. They can be obtained by multiplying the per share values by N, the number of shares acquired at conversion. The resulting option value O of the bond is represented in Equation 3.17, while the intrinsic and floor values of the conversion option (denoted by O_i and O_f, respectively) can be expressed as follows:[7]

$$O_i = \max[0, NS - I_m - M], \tag{3.18}$$

$$O_f = \max[0, \ NS \ - \ PV(I_m \ + \ M)]. \tag{3.19}$$

In graphical terms these latter value functions are no longer partially represented by straight lines that form an angle of $45°$ with the horizontal axis or, in other words, that have a slope equal to 1. As shown in Figure 3.6, they are instead partially represented by parallel lines with a slope equal to N. Their

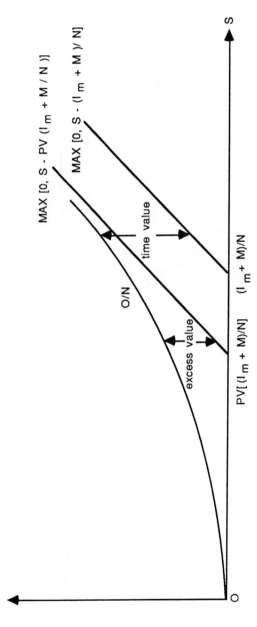

Figure 3.5

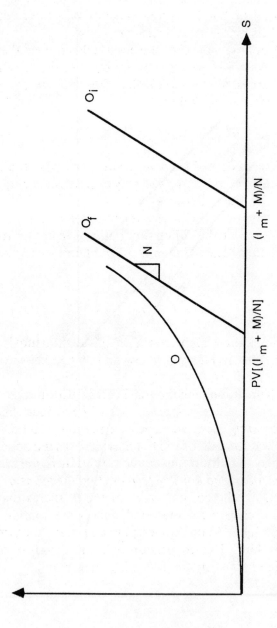

Figure 3.6

intercept with the horizontal axis, however, is still the same. The excess of the bond's option value over its floor value is also amplified by the same factor N.

Once the option value O of the bond is determined then, its total bond value B is obtained by adding it to the investment value I, as expressed in Equation 3.1. We can therefore quantify the bond value as follows:

$$B = I + f(NS, I_m + M, t) \qquad (3.20)$$

Graphically speaking, this comes down to shifting the curve in Figure 3.6 upward in a parallel way over a distance equal to I, as shown in Figure 3.7.

Similarly, if we add the investment value to the intrinsic and floor values of the conversion option, we obtain the intrinsic and floor values B_i and B_f of the bond as a whole:

$$B_i = I + O_i, \qquad (3.21)$$

$$B_f = I + O_f. \qquad (3.22)$$

As shown in Figure 3.7, this again is equivalent to moving the two straight lines in Figure 3.6 upward in a parallel way over a distance equal to I.

Finally, before applying the Black-Scholes formula to convertible bonds in the next section, we will conclude this section by presenting other versions of Equation 3.20 based on the *conversion value* B_c of the bond, which was introduced in Chapter 2. By definition, *the conversion value represents the exchange value of the bond determined by the terms of conversion,* that is, the current value of the N shares that are received in exchange for the bond, minus any margin payments made by the bondholder plus any margin payments received by him. The conversion value is therefore quantitatively determined by the following equation:

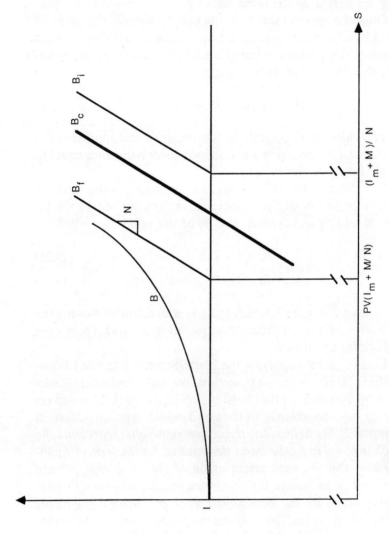

Figure 3.7

$$B_c = NS - M, \tag{3.23}$$

where $M > 0$ (<0) if margin payments are made (received) by the bondholder. The conversion value of a convertible bond therefore depends on the current price of the underlying stock, but is not dependent on either the investment value or the option value of the bond.

It is easy to verify that, *at maturity of the conversion option, the bond's conversion value always coincides with its intrinsic value, unless it is smaller than its investment value.* Indeed, if we denote the stock price at maturity by S_m, the bond's conversion value at maturity B_c^m would be equal to: $B_c^m = NS_m - M$. Therefore, if the conversion value is not smaller than the investment value at maturity, their difference $(NS_m - M) - I_m$ must be greater than or equal to zero. Consequently, the bond's intrinsic value B_i^m at maturity would be equal to: $B_i^m = I_m + \max[0, NS_m - (I_m + M)] = NS_m - M$. As the right-hand sides of the two above equations are identical, the conversion value coincides with the intrinsic value at maturity.

Before maturity, on the other hand, the conversion value can either be greater or smaller than the intrinsic value. This is illustrated in Figure 3.7, where B_c is represented by the bold straight line, which is generally referred to as the *conversion line.* It is parallel to the two sloping straight-line segments of the floor value B_i and the intrinsic value B_f. These line segments represent the values $(I - I_m) + (NS - M)$ and $(I + NS) - PV(I_m + M)$, respectively. Depending on whether the applicable discount rate of the bond is greater or smaller than its coupon rate, I will be smaller or greater than I_m and, therefore, the bold line that represents $B_c = NS - M$ should be above or below the sloping line segment of B_i. At the same time, it can also be shown that, in virtually all cases, the conversion line will always fall below the sloping line segment of

B_f. This latter property can indeed mathematically be expressed by Equation A.2 in Appendix A at the end of this chapter, where its validity in all relevant cases is demonstrated.

In view of Equation 3.23, Equation 3.20 is equivalent to:

$$B = I + f(B_c + M, I_m + M, t). \qquad (3.24)$$

By defining B_c' and I_m' as follows:

$$B_c' = B_c + M, \qquad (3.25)$$

$$I_m' = I_m + M, \qquad (3.26)$$

Equation 3.24 could be simplified to:

$$B = I + f(B_c', I_m', t). \qquad (3.27)$$

Obviously, considering Equation 3.27 as an alternative to Equation 3.24 becomes immaterial in the absence of any side payments. Still other equivalent valuation formulas can be obtained by dividing M, B, I, B_c, I_m, B_c', and I_m' in these equations by the nominal bond value B_n. If the resulting fractions of that nominal value are respectively denoted by m, b, i, b_c, i_m, b_c', and i_m', Equations 3.24 and 3.27 can equivalently be expressed as:

$$b = i + f(b_c + m, i_m + m, t), \qquad (3.28)$$

and

$$b = i + f(b_c', i_m', t). \qquad (3.29)$$

Typically, the conversion option matures at the same time as the convertible bond itself. Under those circumstances, the bond's investment value must coincide at maturity with its redemption value:

$$i_m = v,\qquad(3.30)$$

where v denotes the redemption value as a fraction of the bond's nominal value. Equation 3.28 can accordingly be simplified to

$$b = i + f(b_c + m, v + m, t) = i + f(b_c', v', t),\qquad(3.31)$$

where $b_c' = b_c + m$ and $v' = v + m$. As the redemption value coincides with the nominal value in virtually all cases, v will generally take the value 1 in this relationship. Finally, as a reminder from Chapter 2, let us specify again that the investment value i only depends on the bond's coupon rate c, its redemption value v, the discount rate ρ that applies to its risk-class, and its maturity τ:[8]

$$i = i(c, v, \rho, \tau),\qquad(3.32)$$

where $\tau = t$ if the conversion option expires at maturity of the bond. Equations 3.31 and 3.32 will serve as a starting point for analyzing the properties of option and investment values in Chapter 4. The bond valuation function of Equation 3.31 is graphically represented in Figure 3.8.

In this graph, $b_c' = b_c + m$, rather than the stock price, is plotted along the horizontal axis. For that reason, the conversion value b_c itself is no longer represented by a straight line with slope N, but by a 45° line. This conversion line falls below or above the 45° segment of the intrinsic value, depending on whether the investment value i is greater or smaller than the redemption value v, that is, depending on whether the applicable discount rate is smaller or greater than the bond's coupon rate. The 45° segment of the kinked straight line representing the floor value, on the other hand, will normally fall above the conversion line b_c.

The most important value concepts discussed in this subsection, as well as the formulas that characterize them, are

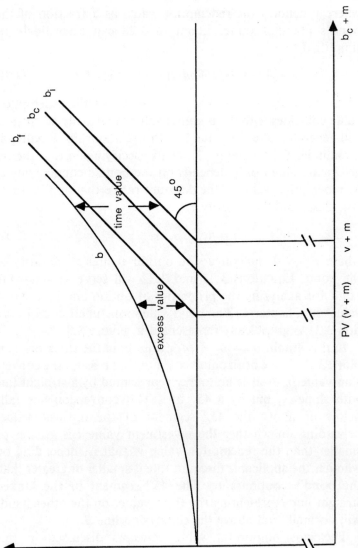

Figure 3.8

summarized below. First, a number of value concepts related to the bond as a whole are shown with name, symbol, and formula. Next follow value concepts related to the bond's conversion option. Finally, some important relationships among some of these value concepts are described.

Value concepts related to the bond as a whole, expressed as a fraction of the nominal bond value B_n

Value concept	Symbol	Formula	
investment value	i	see chapters II and IV	
conversion value	b_c	$b_c = (NS - M)/B_n$	(3.33)
option value	o	$o = f(b_c+m,v+m,t)$	(3.34)
bond value	b	$b = i + f(b_c+m,v+m,t)$	(3.35)
intrinsic value	b_i	$b_i = i + \max(0, b_c- v)$	(3.36)
floor value	b_f	$b_f = i + \max[0, b_c+m-PV(v+m)]$	(3.37)

Value concepts related to the bond's conversion option, expressed as a fraction of the nominal bond value B_n

Value concept	Symbol	Formula	
option value	o	$o = f(b_c+m,v+m,t)$	(3.38)
intrinsic value	o_i	$o_i = \max(0, b_c- v)$	(3.39)
floor value	o_f	$o_f = \max[0, b_c+ m - PV(v+m)]$	(3.40)
time value	o_t	$o_t = f(b_c',v',t) - \max(0, b_c- v)$	(3.41)
excess value	o_e	$o_e = f(b_c',v',t) - \max[0, b_c'- PV(v')]$	(3.42)

It is easy to verify that the following basic relationships can be established among these value concepts:

$$b_i = i + o_i, \tag{3.43}$$

$$b_f = i + o_f. \tag{3.44}$$

$$o = o_f + o_e = o_i + o_t, \tag{3.45}$$

$$b = i + o = b_i + o_t = b_f + o_e. \tag{3.46}$$

We will now further specify the above value functions in the next section by applying the Black-Scholes option valuation formula to the conversion option of convertible bonds.

Applying the Black-Scholes formula to convertible bond valuation

The purpose of this section is to show how convertible bonds can be valued in a more specific way using the Black-Scholes option valuation formula. In principle, this only requires a specification of the bond's option value $o = f(b_c + m, v + m, t)$. Since the Black-Scholes specification for $f(S, E, t)$ is given in Equation 3.11, 3.12, and 3.13, the specification for $f(b_c + m, v + m, t)$ is obtained by substituting $b_c + m$ for S and $v + m$ for E in these equations. This results in the following Black-Scholes formula for the conversion option:

$$o = b_c' \Phi(d_1) - PV(v') \Phi(d_2), \tag{3.47}$$

where

$$d_1 = \frac{\ln(b_c'/v') + (r + .5\sigma^2)t}{\sigma \sqrt{t}}, \tag{3.48}$$

$$d_2 = \frac{\ln(b_c'/v') + (r - .5\sigma^2)t}{\sigma \sqrt{t}}, \tag{3.49}$$

and where $b_c' = b_c + m$ and $v' = v + m$. Once the option value is specified according to the above formulas, Equations 3.35, 3.41, and 3.42 can be used to specify the bond value b, the time value o_t, and the excess value o_e.

A numerical example

To illustrate Equations 3.33 through 3.49, let us consider the example of an investor, John, who wants to figure out the value of a noncallable convertible bond issued by company XYZ, that has a nominal bond value of $1000 and a conversion option with a remaining life of 7 years and 9 months. Based on the principles of straight bond valuation, John has been able to figure out that the current investment value of the bond equals 86 percent of its nominal value. He estimates that σ^2, the volatility of the price of stock XYZ (defined above, "The Black-Scholes Option Valuation Model"), is .16 per year, and considers a continuously compounded risk-free rate of return r equal to 7 percent. Currently, the stock is quoted at $38.25, while the conversion price specified on the bond is $35 per share. Furthermore, the redemption value of bond equals 100 percent of its nominal value. Finally, no margin payments are required at conversion as fraction rule (c) (described in Chapter 2) applies, according to which the number of shares to be received in exchange for the bond is rounded to the nearest smaller integer.

John first needs to figure out the conversion value of the bond. In view of the fraction rule that applies, the number of shares to be received at conversion equals the greatest integer that is smaller than or equal to $1000/$35 = 28.57. This means that $N = 28$, while $v = 1$ and $m = 0$. Consequently, $v' = v = 1$ and $b_c' = b_c = (28)($38.25) = $1,071$ or 107.1 percent of the nominal bond value. The values of d_1 and d_2 can then be calculated as follows:

$$d_1 = \frac{\ln 1.071 + [.07 + (.5)(.16)](7.75)}{\sqrt{(.16)(7.75)}} = 1.1056,$$

$$d_2 = \frac{\ln 1.071 + [.07 - (.5)(.16)](7.75)}{\sqrt{(.16)(7.75)}} = -0.008.$$

From the table in Appendix B at the end of this chapter, it can be seen that $\Phi(d_1)$ and $\Phi(d_2)$ have approximate values of .8643 and .5, respectively. By means of a statistical hand calculator it is easy to verify that, more accurately, $\Phi(d_1) = .8655$ and $\Phi(d_2) = .4968$. By substituting these values in Equation 3.47, the following value can be derived for the bond's conversion option:

$$o = (1.071)(.8655) - (.4968)\,e^{-(.07)(7.75)}$$

$$= 0.6382.$$

This means that the bond's option value is 63.82 percent of its nominal value, or \$638.20.

Next, let us use Equations 3.39 and 3.40 to determine the intrinsic value o_i and the floor value o_f of the conversion option:

$$o_i = \max(0, 1.071 - 1) = 7.1\%$$

$$o_f = \max[0, 1.071 - e^{-(.07)(7.75)}] = 48.97\%$$

Finally, Equations 3.43 through 3.46 imply that

$$o_t = o - o_i = 63.82\% - 7.1\% = 56.72\%$$
(option's time value)

$$o_e = o - o_f = 63.82\% - 48.97\% = 14.85\%$$
(option's excess value)

$$b_i = i + o_i = 86\% + 7.1\% = 93.1\%$$
(bond's intrinsic value)

$$b_f = i + o_f = 86\% + 48.97\% = 134.97\%$$

(bond's floor value)

$$b = i + o = 86\% + 63.82\% = 149.82\%$$

(bond value)

All the above values are expressed as a percentage of the nominal bond value. They can also be expressed in dollar terms, simply by multiplying these percentages by $1000.

Arbitrage

If convertible bonds are priced in the marketplace in conformity with the principles explained in this chapter, it is not possible to make arbitrage profits from simultaneous transactions in the convertible bond market and in the stock market. In reality, however, convertible bonds are often mispriced relative to their underlying stock, which sometimes creates opportunities for realizing immediately foreseeable, risk-free profits. Such an opportunity may, for example, arise when a convertible bond sells at a price below its floor value B_f. Such a bond would obviously be a real bargain if this floor value coincides with the bond's investment value I, as its conversion option would then in fact have a negative price. More interesting, however, is the case in which the floor value exceeds the investment value, and the bond price falls in between. Risk-free profits could then be realized by buying the bond, and by shorting a number of shares of the underlying stock equal to the number N of shares into which the bond can be converted. If the floor value exceeds the investment value, Equations 3.19 and 3.22 imply that it can be determined as follows:

$$B_f = I + NS - PV(I_m + M).$$

If the bond sells at a discount Δ relative to this floor value, if the stock is shorted at a price S per share, and if transaction costs are ignored, buying the bond and shorting N shares would immediately result in the following cash flow:

$$NS - (B_f - \Delta) = NS - [I + NS - PV(I_m + M) - \Delta],$$
$$= PV(M) - [I - PV(I_m)] + \Delta.$$

The short position can be closed out by converting the bond into N shares of common stock at the expiration date of the conversion option. This conversion may result in a cash flow that corresponds to a side payment M with a present value equal to $- PV(M)$. Before maturity, however, coupon interests are earned on the bond, with a total present value equal to $I - PV(I_m)$. The present value of all these cash flows equals $NS - (B_f - \Delta) - PV(M) + [I - PV(I_m)]$, which can be shown to equal Δ in view of the above relationships. This present value may be considered the risk-free arbitrage profit. In principle, it could be fully realized at the present time by buying Treasury bills with a total redemption value equal to M, and by borrowing against all future interest income on the bond. In practice, however, arbitrageurs would incur transaction costs, and realized profit would therefore be less than Δ. For small discounts Δ, it might even be negative. As a rule, therefore, this kind of arbitrage activities only pays when convertible bonds sell at a sufficiently large discount relative to their floor value.

The conversion premium and the premium over investment value

The concepts of *conversion premium* and *premium over investment value* are very commonly used in professional practice. They play an important role in the conventional methods of selecting convertible bonds. It would therefore be interesting to find out how these traditional concepts fit in with modern option theory.

To start with, let us consider the conversion premium first. This premium is defined as *the relative amount by which the bond value exceeds the conversion value,* that is, the difference between the bond value and the conversion value, as a fraction of the latter. Whereas the conversion value corresponds to the right of converting the bond immediately, the conversion premium corresponds to the right to delay the conversion—or not to convert the bond at all—while receiving interest payments as long as the conversion option is not exercised. According to the above definition, we can express the conversion premium as the following ratio:

$$\frac{b - b_c}{b_c}. \tag{3.50}$$

The numerator in this expression will be referred to as the *dollar value* of the conversion premium (expressed as a fraction of the nominal bond value). This dollar value can be either greater or smaller than the time value of the conversion option, *depending on whether the bond's intrinsic value is greater or smaller than its conversion value.* Thus, in the example described two sections previously, the dollar value of the conversion premium should be smaller than the option's time value, which was equal to 56.72 percent of the nominal bond value, as the bond's intrinsic value of 93.1 percent is smaller than its conversion value of 107.1 percent. This indeed is correct, as the dollar value of the premium is equal to $b - b_c = 149.82$ percent $- 107.1$ percent $= 42.72$ percent of the nominal value. The conversion premium itself equals $42.72/107.1 = 39.89$ percent. This means that an investor buying this convertible bond should be willing to pay a price that exceeds the conversion value by 39.89 percent, to account for the fact that he is entitled to delay or forego any conversion, while receiving interest payments as long as the conversion has not taken place.

Also observe the fact that the option's time value exceeds the dollar value of the premium by an amount of 56.72 percent − 42.72 percent = 14 percent of the nominal value, which is exactly equal to the difference between the conversion value and the intrinsic value (107.1 percent − 93.1 percent = 14 percent). This is no coincidence, but rather a special application of the following general relationship between the premium's dollar amount $b - b_c$ and the option's time value o_t:

$$b - b_c = o_t + (b_i - b_c). \tag{3.51}$$

The other concept used in professional practice is the premium over investment value which, by definition, equals *the relative amount by which the bond value exceeds the investment value*. This premium, therefore, can be expressed as the ratio:

$$\frac{b - i}{i} \tag{3.52}$$

The numerator of Equation 3.52 could again be referred to as the premium's dollar value, as a fraction of the nominal bond value. In view of Equation 3.46, *this dollar value coincides with the option value of the bond*:

$$b - i = o \tag{3.53}$$

The premium over investment value, therefore, is nothing but a premium that the convertible bond investor has to pay for the privilege of the conversion option. In the example described two sections previously, it turns out to be 63.82/86 = 74.21 percent. This means that an investor who buys this convertible bond should be willing to pay a price that is 74.21 percent greater than the value of the bond without any conversion feature.

The conversion premium and the premium over investment value are often used as criteria for selecting convertible bonds, in which case the actual market price is substituted for the bond value *b* in Equations 3.50 and 3.52. The idea is that, all other things being equal, the smaller the premiums that one has to pay as an investor the better. Other things are seldom equal, however, as two bonds with different premiums will generally differ in their basic characteristics as well. This means that any investor has to weigh the size of the premiums against the benefits that he receives for paying them. For example, one of the basic characteristics to be considered in this comparison is the remaining life of the conversion option. Indeed, the longer the maturity the higher both premiums, as at least part of these premiums must be paid as a compensation for the fact that the conversion can be delayed until the conversion option expires. It would therefore not be very meaningful to compare different convertible bonds on the basis of their premiums, without taking into account at the same time the respective maturities of their conversion options.

One other reason why these premiums should not be used as isolated criteria is that the criteria may be in conflict with each other. Indeed, all other things being equal, the premium over investment value of a convertible bond will increase, and its conversion premium will decrease in response to an increase in the price of its underlying stock. Therefore, a rule needs to be specified about the way in which these criteria should be applied to solve such a conflict.

The conclusion from all this is that, although the premiums

as such give some indication as to the merits of one convertible bond over another, they fail to provide satisfactory answers to some basic questions. The selection problem will be extensively discussed in Chapter 4, where it is approached in a more fundamental way based on the expected bond return as a decision criterion.

Some practical considerations

The example above ("A Numerical Example") shows us how the Black-Scholes valuation formula can be used to determine the value of convertible bonds in an elegant way. It should be clearly understood, however, that this value is theoretical in nature and that it only applies under certain assumptions. Some of these assumptions relate to the Black-Scholes option valuation formula itself; others relate to the applicability of option theory to convertible bond valuation. Some of these assumptions could be relaxed without complicating the analysis too much, while others were more or less indispensible for deriving a suitable valuation formula from call option theory.

Obviously, the actual price will normally differ somewhat from this theoretical value. One reason for this is that, generally speaking, the assumptions underlying the theoretical formula will be met only to a certain degree. A second reason is that, even when all assumptions fully apply, the market price level of any convertible bond is determined by supply and demand decisions that need not be based on the theoretical formula. In other words, even when the theoretical formula would provide the "correct" price for that bond, it could still be temporarily overvalued or undervalued in the marketplace. And even in the most unlikely event that all market participants would base their decisions on the Black-Scholes formula, they would undoubtedly assume different degrees of volatility of the underlying stock price, which would result in many different bond value estimates made by these participants. The actual bond price would then at best be some kind of average of all these individual estimates, which in turn can only be considered approximations of the market price.

This discrepancy between theoretical and market values could be exploited to spot undervalued and overvalued convertible bonds in the marketplace, and to reshuffle one's portfolio of convertible bonds accordingly. As a reliable estimate of the stock's volatility is of critical importance in this connection, it may pay to determine a whole range of Black-Scholes bond values that corresponds to a suitable confidence interval of that volatility. The position of the actual market price relative to such a range would then be an important factor in determining whether any bond is more likely to be undervalued than overvalued, or vice versa. It should be noted, however, that an empirical study by MacBeth and Merville (1980) has shown that there exists some bias in the Black-Scholes option valuation formula, in that it has a tendency to overvalue out-of-the-money call options and to undervalue in-the-money call options. Additional types of bias were found in other studies, such as those by Black and Scholes (1972) and by Geske and Roll (1984). The same types of bias can obviously also be expected to exist in the Black-Scholes valuation of convertible bonds. This means that one should be extremely careful in interpreting any deviation of the market price of a call option or a convertible bond from its Black-Scholes value. As we do not generally see actual market prices tending toward the Black-Scholes values, the latter cannot be interpreted as equilibrium prices from which the market prices are a temporary deviation. Therefore, if some systematic discrepancy exists between market prices and corresponding Black-Scholes values, we have no reason to believe that something is wrong with the market. The right conclusion is more likely to be that the Black-Scholes model is misspecified to some degree and needs improvement. What could be done until a better model is developed is to measure the bias and to take it into account in an explicit way, before drawing any conclusions with respect to whether call options and convertible bonds are overvalued or undervalued in the marketplace.

Instead of using the Black-Scholes values as a reference value to identify incorrectly priced bonds, they can also be used to estimate the value implicitly assigned by the market to special bond features. Assume, for example, that for a particular bond all assumptions underlying the model of this chapter are reasonably well satisfied, except the noncallability assumption. In that case, the difference between the Black-Scholes value and the market price of the bond constitutes a good estimate of the amount by which the bond value is discounted by the market in view of its callability.

Still another application of the Black-Scholes formula is the determination of the degree of volatility that is implied by the bond's market price, that is, the value of σ^2 for which the Black-Scholes value equals the market price. This can be done by a trial-and-error procedure or by a suitable computer program. If, for example, the convertible bond described previously ("A Numerical Example") were traded at 145 percent instead of 149.82 percent of its nominal value, the implicit volatility of the stock would be approximately .1055 instead of .16. If regular call options are traded in the option market that have the same underlying stock as the convertible bond under consideration, one may be tempted to derive additional estimates of σ^2 from call option prices. It should be kept in mind, however, that different volatilities generally apply to a convertible bond and to any call option on its underlying stock, in view of the fact that a convertible bond typically has a much longer duration than a call option. Volatilities of a stock implied by call options prices should therefore not be compared to volatilities derived from convertible bond prices. On the other hand, one could consider the volatility of a stock implied by the price of a given convertible bond, in the valuation of any other with the same underlying stock, provided they have approximately the same maturity.

A more direct method of estimating the stock's volatility is to determine historical values of σ^2 for the given stock. One simply observes historical stock prices for some period of time in the recent past, and then finds the variance per unit of time of the continuously compounded rate of return on the stock. Although, in principle, it is the stock's *future* volatility that must be estimated, its past volatility can be used as a reasonable approximation of its future volatility, unless special circumstances or expectations about the future course of events are believed to change the stock's degree of volatility over time.

To illustrate this more direct method, consider a stock with the following closing prices at the end of each week, for a total period of 10 weeks:

week (t)	closing price(S_t)	continuously compounded weekly return (ρ_t)
0	42 3/8	—
1	45 1/8	6.29%
2	41 1/2	−8.37%
3	39	−6.21%
4	40 3/4	4.39%
5	37 5/8	−7.98%
6	33	−13.12%
7	32 1/8	−2.69%
8	35	8.57%
9	37 1/4	6.23%
10	39	4.59%

For each week t, the continuously compounded weekly return ρ_t, that appears in the third column, is determined by the following formula:

$$\rho_t = \ln(S_t/S_{t-1}). \tag{3.54}$$

The sample variance of all these returns is defined by

$$\sigma^2 = \frac{\sum\limits_{t=1}^{n} (\rho_t - \bar{\rho})^2}{n - 1}, \tag{3.55}$$

where n stands for the total number of observed returns, and where $\bar{\rho}$ represents the mean of all returns, defined by

$$\bar{\rho} = \frac{1}{n} \sum\limits_{t=1}^{n} \rho_t. \tag{3.56}$$

Using a value of n equal to 10, it is easy to verify that in the above example $\bar{\rho} = -.83$ percent per week, and that $\sigma^2 = .006$ on a weekly basis. By multiplying these figures by 52, we obtain an annualized average rate of return of -43.16 percent and an annualized variance equal to .31. Based on these figures, one should therefore substitute a value of .31 for σ^2 in the formula of Black and Scholes.

The procedure, according to which the annualized variance can be found simply by multiplying the weekly variance by 52, is in fact based (1) on the assumption that all observed returns are uncorrelated and (2) on the assumption that the weekly variance is constant over time. These assumptions are not likely to be satisfied for small samples like the one considered in the above example. That is just one reason why one should prefer samples with a large number of observations. A second reason is that sample variances of large samples are much more accurate estimates of the population variance than sample variances of small samples. Large samples are easily obtained by considering daily instead of weekly returns, over a sufficiently long period of time. The observation of daily returns also has the added benefit that they represent a much better approximation of the constantly changing, continuously compounded rate of return than do weekly rates, which again leads to more accurate estimates of σ^2. Furthermore, it is important to stress that the observed data should be as recent as possible, as more recent data are normally better a simulation of the future than older data. Finally, whereas we pointed out that the sample period should be large enough to guarantee a large enough sample, one should at the same time keep it small enough to be confident that the assumption of a constant variance is reasonably well satisfied.

APPENDIX A: MARGIN PAYMENTS
AND EARLY CONVERSION

In this appendix, we analyze the impact of margin payments on the possibility of early voluntary conversion. Let us start by pointing out that the conversion option, contrary to a regular call option or warrant, has no constant exercise price. As pointed out earlier in this chapter, the exercise price of the option to convert the bond into N shares equals the amount of the side payments plus the bond's investment value at the time of conversion. Since the investment value changes over time, the exercise prices that correspond to different conversion times will be different as well. In particular, when the bond is converted at maturity, the total exercise price equals $I_m + M$, whereas the total exercise price would be $I + M$ when the bond is converted at the present time.

In this connection, a distinction must be made between two important cases. First, consider the case in which the relevant discount rate of the bond is less than or equal to its coupon rate. In this case, we know from straight bond theory that the current investment value I of the bond must be greater than or equal to its investment value at maturity I_m. Consequently,

$$I + M \geqslant I_m + M > PV(I_m + M), \qquad (A.1)$$

which means that the total exercise price, to be paid when the bond is converted at the present time, is greater than the present value of the total exercise price to be paid when conversion takes place at maturity. As a consequence, the profit $NS - (I + M)$ that can be made by converting the bond at the present time would be smaller than the floor value $NS - PV(I_m + M)$ of the conversion option. Under those circumstances, the bondholder should not convert the bond before the expiration date of the conversion option, as he would be better off by selling it.

Second, consider the case in which the applicable discount rate of the bond is greater than its coupon rate. In this case $I < I_m$, so that the current exercise price is smaller this time than the exercise price at maturity. The main question is, however, whether or not the current exercise price is greater than or equal to the present value of the exercise price at maturity, that is, whether or not

$$I + M \geqslant PV(I_m + M). \qquad (A.2)$$

If this condition is met, the profit $NS - (I + M)$ derived from immediate conversion would be smaller than or equal to the floor value $NS - PV(I_m + M)$ of the bond's conversion option, and therefore smaller than the option value itself. Under those circumstances, therefore, the bondholder would be better off again by selling the bond than by converting it.

If, on the other hand, condition A.2 is not met, the benefit derived from immediate conversion would be greater than the floor value of the conversion option, and therefore it could even be greater than the bond's option value. If and when this occurs, early conversion could be justified.

Condition A.2 is equivalent to

$$I - PV(I_m) \geqslant PV(M) - M. \tag{A.3}$$

The left-hand side of this inequality is equal to the present value of the coupon payments C that are received during the period from the present time up to maturity. As such it is always nonnegative, while the right-hand side is always nonpositive if $M \geqslant 0$.

Consequently, this inequality is always satisfied, and therefore early conversion is not in the best interest of the bondholder, if $M \geqslant 0$, that is, if there are no side payments or if some amount of money has to be paid by the bondholder to the issuing company at the time of conversion. If, on the other hand, the bondholder receives some side payments at conversion from the company, M would be negative and condition A.3 would be violated for a large enough absolute value of M. In the rare cases in which negative side payments are made, however, they reflect adjustments that must be made in application of the fraction rules that were discussed in Chapter 2. As these adjustments are normally very small, we can conclude that, for all practical purposes, condition A.3 is always met. Therefore, *margin payments will normally never lead to early conversion.*

APPENDIX B: VALUES OF Φ(x) FOR SELECTED VALUES OF x

x	Φ(x)	x	Φ(x)	x	Φ(x)
−1.75	.0401	−0.55	.2912	0.65	.7422
−1.70	.0446	−0.50	.3085	0.70	.7580
−1.65	.0495	−0.45	.3264	0.75	.7734
−1.60	.0548	−0.40	.3446	0.80	.7881
−1.55	.0606	−0.35	.3632	0.85	.8023
−1.50	.0668	−0.30	.3821	0.90	.8159
−1.45	.0735	−0.25	.4013	0.95	.8289
−1.40	.0808	−0.20	.4207	1.00	.8413
−1.35	.0885	−0.15	.4404	1.05	.8531
−1.30	.0968	−0.10	.4602	1.10	.8643
−1.25	.1057	−0.05	.4801	1.15	.8749
−1.20	.1151	0.00	.5000	1.20	.8849
−1.15	.1251	0.05	.5199	1.25	.8944
−1.10	.1357	0.10	.5398	1.30	.9032
−1.05	.1469	0.15	.5596	1.35	.9115
−1.00	.1587	0.20	.5793	1.40	.9192
−0.95	.1711	0.25	.5987	1.45	.9265
−0.90	.1841	0.30	.6179	1.50	.9332
−0.85	.1977	0.35	.6368	1.55	.9394
−0.80	.2119	0.40	.6554	1.60	.9452
−0.75	.2266	0.45	.6736	1.65	.9505
−0.70	.2420	0.50	.6915	1.70	.9554
−0.65	.2578	0.55	.7088	1.75	.9599
−0.60	.2743	0.60	.7257	1.80	.9641

NOTES

1. More in particular, new stock is created at the time of conversion, which has a diluting effect on the value of the existing stock. On the other hand, it is also true that the existing and new shares represent a larger part of the value of the firm than did the existing stock before the conversion. Consequently, conversion of all outstanding bond issues will generally affect the stock price level. In such a case, the relevant stock price to consider at the time of conversion is the new adjusted price, that fully reflects this change in the capital structure of the issuing company. If only a relatively small number of bonds are converted by a single investor, the corresponding impact on the stock price level will be negligibly small.

2. There exists an exception to this rule. Namely, it can be shown that it may sometimes pay to exercise a call option just prior to an ex-dividend date for the underlying stock. The reason is that when the option is exercised after that date, the option holder is no longer entitled to receive the dividend. Similarly, when bonds are converted into stock, no compensation is given for any dilution of the value of the stock due to *cash dividend* payments in the past. Usually, however, option values and conversion values of convertible bonds are protected against other dilutions of stock value, such as *stock dividends* and *stock splits*. In this text, we will generally ignore complications caused by cash dividend payments, except where stated otherwise.

3. The main assumptions are: (1) the stock price follows a random walk and the continuously compounded return on the stock is normally distributed; (2) the rate of interest is constant until the option's maturity date; (3) there are no transaction costs, no taxes, and no penalties for short selling; (4) the stock does not pay any dividend during the life of the option.

4. Formally speaking, $\Phi(x)$ corresponds to the area under the curve of the standardized normal probability distribution to the left of x, which is mathematically expressed by the following integral:

$$\Phi(x) = (2\pi)^{-1/2} \int_{-\infty}^{x} e^{-y^2/2} \, dy.$$

5. In the absence of any cash dividend payments, we could equivalently define the stock's volatility as the variance per unit of time of the natural logarithm of the stock price. Indeed, if ρ represents the continuously compounded rate of return on the stock, and if P represents the future stock price one period of time from now, then $P = Se^\rho$. This implies that $\rho = \ln(P/S) = \ln(P) - \ln(S)$. Since the nonstochastic parameter S has a zero variance, ρ and $\ln(P)$ must have the same variance.

6. This assumption of a constant risk-free rate of interest r is similar to the assumption of a constant discount rate ρ made in Chapter 2. Both these rates are therefore assumed to have the same level for different periods of time. This comes down to assuming that the yield curve for risk-free securities, or for straight bonds of any particular risk-class, is flat. However, such an assumption does *not* exclude the possibility that this flat yield curve will shift up or down over time. In other words, it still makes sense to consider changes in r or ρ over time, as we shall do in Chapter 4 when determining the sensitivity of a convertible bond's value to such changes. The analysis of this text can theoretically be extended to include different interest rate levels for different periods of time, but only at the expense of increased complexity and reduced practical applicability.

7. Note that the present values of the investment value I_m and the margin payment M, that show up in Equation 3.19 as well as in the convertible bond version of the Black-Scholes formula, should theoretically be determined on the basis of discount rates ρ and r, respectively. However, the use of two different discount rates in the Black-Scholes formula considerably complicates the analysis. For the sake of simplicity, therefore, the present values of I_m and M will be discounted at the same rate throughout most of the text. Such a simplification can indeed be expected to lead to good approximate results for all bonds with a sufficiently low risk premium, that is, for all bonds of good enough quality.

8. It is implicitly assumed throughout this text that the investment value i does not depend on the stock price S or the conversion value b_c. This comes down to assuming that stock price movements have no impact on the value of the company's outstanding debt.

The reason why such an impact may exist is that stock price movements affect the value of the company's equity, and therefore also the financial leverage of the company. This in turn will have an impact on the credit risk of its outstanding debt. Changes in the credit risk that are large enough will cause a revision of its bond ratings by *Standard & Poor's* or *Moody's*, which in turn affects the value of its bonds outstanding. In theory, therefore, this value is an increasing function of the stock price, all other things being equal. As long as the company has an excellent credit rating, however, only major setbacks will induce a downward revision of that rating, and will therefore negatively affect the value of outstanding bond issues. As long as we consider convertible bonds of sufficient quality, issued by companies with a relatively stable debt-equity ratio, the dependency of their value on the stock price is negligible and can therefore be ignored for practical purposes. A lucid explanation of the role of credit risk in the valuation of debt can be found in Chapter 19 of Garbade (1982).

4

Selection of
Convertible Bonds

INTRODUCTION

A major decision problem faced by security investors relates to
the selection of the specific securities to invest in, and to the allocation of scarce investment capital to these specific securities. In
other words, all security investors have to determine how much
money to invest in which securities. They obviously have to try to
find the best possible answer to these questions, and to select their
investment portfolio accordingly. Harry M. Markowitz (1952,
1959) was the first to systematically analyze the problem of portfolio selection in a rigorous way. Under the assumptions of the
portfolio selection model that he developed, the optimal portfolio
consists of a combination of a risk-free security (which for practical purposes is usually assumed to be a U.S. Treasury security
with suitable maturity) and some portfolio of risky securities that
is to be specified within the framework of the model.

Markowitz's model fully exploits the possibilities of reducing the portfolio risk through *diversification*, that is, through
combining a wide variety of different securities in a single
portfolio. By building a well-diversified portfolio, any investor

can reduce his exposure to risk without reducing at the same time the expected return on his investment. In more popular terms, diversification corresponds to not putting all of one's eggs in the same basket. It is clear that any circumstance that adversely affects one security in a portfolio need not have a negative effect on other securities in that portfolio.

Note that if we apply Markowitz's model to convertible bonds, any convertible bond portfolio that is optimal within the class of convertible bonds will generally not be optimal within a larger class of secutities or risky assets. The reason for this is that the possibilities of diversifying away portfolio risk are larger within larger categories of assets. With the exception of mutual funds that invest exclusively in convertible bonds, institutional and other investors usually buy convertible bonds as part of a larger portfolio, such as a stock or bond fund. In most cases, therefore, the problem of selecting an optimal portfolio of convertible bonds is only part of a larger problem, according to which an optimal portfolio is to be determined for whatever larger category of capital assets is considered by the investor.

Although Markowitz's model is one of the best theoretical models of portfolio selection around, it cannot easily be applied to practical portfolio management if a large number of securities is considered. For any security considered, the model requires the estimation of its expected return, the standard deviation of its return, and the covariances between its return and the returns of all other securities. If n different securities are involved, the model therefore requires the estimation of n expected rates of return, n standard deviations, and $n(n - 1)/2$ covariances. In total, $n(n + 3)/2$ parameters must be estimated. For example, if 100 securities are considered, 5150 different parameters must be estimated, 4950 of which are covariances. The collection and processing of the data underlying that many estimates is very expensive and time-consuming, which prevents Markowitz's model from being very practical.

For that reason, Sharpe (1963) developed a simplified version of this model that drastically reduces the number of parameters to be estimated. His *single-index model* is based on observed co-movements between individual security prices and the value of the market portfolio of all securities. The essence of this model is a linear relationship between the expected return on any individual security and the expected return on the market portfolio, known as the *characteristic line* of that security. The observed returns will normally deviate from that characteristic line by some residual terms. The single-index model will produce exactly the same results as Markowitz's model, provided that the residuals of all individual securities are perfectly *uncorrelated* with each other. The simplification introduced by Sharpe results from the assumption that the pairwise covariances of the individual security returns can be explained completely by their correlation with the return on the market portfolio. Under this assumption we no longer need to consider $n(n-1)/2$ pairwise covariances of the security returns, but only n covariances of the security returns with the market return. In the above example of 100 securities, this reduces the number of covariances to be estimated from 4950 to 100. To the degree that the residuals are correlated with each other and with the market return, the results from the single-index model will be only an approximation of the results obtained within Markowitz's model. Any existing correlation among the residuals, and between the residuals and the market return, can sometimes be reduced by considering additional important factors underlying the individual security returns, other than the return on the market as a whole. Models based on more than one factor are in this connection referred to as *multi-index* models.

Even when the cost of analysis can drastically be reduced by this simplified approach, it may nevertheless still be considerable. Furthermore, the results are only as reliable as the estimates from which they are derived. One should also keep in mind that the parameters to be estimated reflect the investor's expectations about *future* security returns, whereas the estimates themselves are usually based on observed data from the *past*. To the degree that the behavior of the security returns cannot be extrapolated to the future, such estimates may actually not be reliable and may need to be corrected for whatever new circumstances may condition the future course of both the individual returns and the market return.

Independently of whether Markowitz's full covariance approach or Sharpe's simplified approach is taken, the optimal portfolio of risky securities may contain just too many securities to be practically manageable, in view of the high transaction costs of adjusting large portfolios to changing conditions. Also, to the degree that the optimal solution calls for very small amounts of money to be invested in certain securities, that solution may not be feasible in view of the limited divisibility of these securities. Convertible bonds, for example, are always issued in denominations of at least $1000. Any investment of less than $1000 in such a bond, called for by the optimal solution, therefore cannot be considered if the bond sells above par.

For all these reasons, the theoretical solutions provided by the portfolio models discussed above are often difficult and/or expensive to determine and to implement in practice, if a large number of securities is involved. The selection of only a limited number of securities is therefore often a practical necessity. This explains why most portfolio managers and investors typically select a relatively small number of "promising" securities, before making any decision as to how to distribute their investment capital among these preselected securities.

Both the preselection and the allocation of capital can be determined by assigning ranks to the different securities on the basis of certain criteria. As such ranking procedures quite commonly underly investment decisions in professional practice, it will be shown in the rest of this chapter how convertible bonds can be selected by means of a meaningful ranking procedure, such that better-ranked bonds can be considered more promising investment vehicles in light of the investor's expectations. The particular ranking procedure described in this chapter is based on the single most important criterion, namely the expected bond return. It is shown how expected bond returns can be derived from the investor's expectations about the behavior of the stock market as a whole, and about the future course of interest rates. Once ranks are assigned, the investment capital may be allocated among an adequate number of bonds that are expected to outperform all other bonds. That number should be large enough to diversify away a substantial part of the portfolio risk, and it should at the same time be small enough to keep the portfolio manageable without unduly high transaction costs. Obviously, more money should be allocated to bonds with higher ranks than to bonds with lower ranks.

This approach is obviously incomplete, unless the portfolio risk is given due consideration as well. This can be done simply by determining, for each bond, three different rates of return: one that is based on optimistic assumptions, one that is based on pessimistic assumptions, and one that is based on the most likely conditions to prevail. The risk associated with any given convertible bond could be determined by assigning subjective probabilities of occurrence to its optimistic, pessimistic, and most likely rate of return, and by considering the corresponding probability distribution of its return. Each bond can then be assigned a unique rank based not only on the relative magnitude of the mean of its probability distribution, but also on the relative magnitude of its standard deviation as a measure of the risk involved.

The best theoretical way of handling risk is nevertheless provided by the portfolio approach, in that it takes fully into account the possibility of reducing risk through diversification. In view of its practical drawbacks and its complexity, however, we will not focus on the portfolio approach in this text. The interested reader is referred to the section at the end of this chapter ("The Risk Factor"), in which this approach to convertible bond selection is briefly outlined on the basis of the results from the previous sections. We will instead focus on the derivation of the expected bond returns. This derivation is partly based on the properties of the investment value of a convertible bond and partly on the properties of its option value, both of which are discussed in the next section ("Basic Properties of Investment and Option Values").

Before discussing these properties, however, a final word is in order on the convertible bond pricing mechanism. We assume in all sections that convertible bonds are *correctly* priced in the marketplace. They may be undervalued or overvalued to the degree that the convertible bond market is *inefficient*, that is, to the degree that this market is slow in adjusting prices to new information that becomes available to the general public. Although the convertible bond market is most likely not as efficient as the stock market or as the straight bond market, we will consider it efficient enough to justify the assumption that, by and large, convertible bonds are correctly priced most of the time.

The convertible bond market is undoubtedly less efficient than the stock market or the straight bond market for a number of reasons. First, it takes a lot of expertise and research to find the best opportunities in view of the hybrid character of the convertible bond, so that only a relatively small number of investors can actively trace the bargains. Second, it is not as easy for the unsophisticated investor to receive expert advice on convertible bonds from brokerage houses or investment advisers, as it is to receive advice on stocks and straight bonds. In addition, specific convertible bonds are by far not as frequently recommended by them as specific stocks or straight bonds. Third, trading volume in the convertible market is much smaller than in the stock market or in the straight bond market, except for only the most actively traded convertibles. This is due to the fact that the total dollar value of all outstanding convertible bonds is far less than the dollar value of all outstanding stocks or straight bonds.

To the degree that the market is inefficient, it may pay to trace the undervalued bonds. One conceivable way of finding undervalued convertible bonds consists of using the Black-Scholes formula as a yardstick to determine whether the market has mispriced any particular convertible bonds that fit reasonably well into the Black-Scholes framework. A few words of caution are in order here, however. As we pointed out in Chapter 3, empirical studies have shown that the Black-Scholes model shows different kinds of bias in the way in which it values call options. Similar kinds of bias can therefore also be expected to exist in applying the Black-Scholes formula to convertible bonds. This means that convertible bonds that seem to be undervalued on the basis of the Black-Scholes formula may in fact turn out to be overvalued. Consequently, any existing bias should first be measured and the Black-Scholes values should be adjusted accordingly, before comparing them with the actual market prices. Furthermore, convertible bonds may be priced below the Black-Scholes value because of special features of those bonds that make them less attractive to investors. A good example of this is the callability feature that is not explicitly taken into account by the Black-Scholes model. Finally, a convertible bond may seemingly be undervalued when its price is compared to its Black-Scholes value, because the latter was derived from too high an estimate of the volatility of its underlying stock.

In principle, we believe that attempts to trace undervalued securities make a lot of sense in less efficient markets. In practice, however, such an approach can only lead to superior returns if mispriced securities are detected by means of a reliable yardstick. In view of the above problems associated with the use of the Black-Scholes value as a yardstick, we will not take this approach to convertible bond selection in the sections below. As pointed out above, we will instead assume, as a working hypothesis, that the convertible bond market is sufficiently efficient to consider convertible bonds to be correctly priced, unless there is clear evidence to the contrary. It will be shown that under this assumption the volatility of any underlying stock no longer needs to be estimated from historical data, but can easily be derived from the price quotation of the convertible bond. If this volatility turns out to be implausibly low, one may have reason to presume that the bond in question is seriously undervalued.

BASIC PROPERTIES OF INVESTMENT AND OPTION VALUES

In this section we will completely rely on the Black-Scholes formula for deriving some basic properties that are useful in determining the return on a convertible bond, given certain changes in the values of the exogenous parameters underlying the valuation model of Chapter 3. The general format of the convertible bond valuation formula introduced in that chapter, with full indication of all parameters involved, looked as follows:

$$b = i(c, v, \rho, \tau) + f(b_c + m, i_m + m, \sigma, r, t) \qquad (4.1)$$

where

$$i_m = i(c, v, \rho, \tau - t) \qquad (4.2)$$

and

$$b_c = \frac{NS - M}{B_n} \qquad (4.3)$$

As can be seen from this format, there are in total 11 basic parameters in that model, namely the coupon rate c, the redemption value v as a fraction of the nominal bond value, the continuously compounded discount rate ρ that is appropriate for the bond's risk class, the remaining life of the bond represented by the symbol τ, the number N of shares of the underlying stock that can be obtained at conversion, the nominal bond value B_n, the stock price S, any margin payments M to be paid by the bondholder at conversion, the volatility σ^2 of the stock, the risk-free rate of interest r, and the remaining life t of the conversion option. The investment value depends on only the first four of these parameters, whereas the option value depends on all of them. In this section, we first analyze the investment value, and then study the properties of the option value based on its Black-Scholes specification. The properties of the bond value as a whole will be considered in the next section, where we also derive the expected bond returns on the basis of which convertible bonds can be ranked.

Basic properties of the investment value

Let the unit of time correspond to the duration of a coupon period and let us assume, for the sake of simplicity, that the present time coincides with the beginning of a new coupon period. Then we know from Chapter 2 that the investment value is determined by Equation 2.1 in terms of the discount rate ρ '. It can equivalently be determined in terms of the continuously compounded discount rate ρ by the following formulas:

$$i = c \sum_{k=1}^{\tau} e^{-\rho k} + v e^{-\rho \tau} \tag{4.4}$$

$$= \frac{c}{e^{\rho} - 1} + \left[v - \frac{c}{e^{\rho} - 1} \right] e^{-\rho \tau} \tag{4.5}$$

To the degree that the redemption value differs from the nominal value, that is, to the degree that v differs from 1, it is sometimes more useful to express the coupon payment as a fraction of the redemption value than of the nominal value. If we denote this fraction by c ', the relationship between c and c ' can be formulated as follows:

$$c' = c/v. \tag{4.6}$$

The term $e^{\rho} - 1$ in Equation 4.5 is nothing more than the discount rate ρ ' compounded once per unit of time (once per coupon period), that is equivalent to the continuously compounded discount rate ρ. The equivalency condition indeed is:

$$1 + \rho' = e^{\rho}. \tag{4.7}$$

The right side of this equation expresses the terminal value, at the end of one coupon period, of one dollar invested at a continuously compounded rate of interest equal to ρ, while the left side expresses the terminal value of one dollar invested at a rate of interest equal to ρ ' when compounding takes place once per coupon period. When substituting $1 + \rho'$ for e^{ρ} in Equations 4.4 and 4.5, we obtain the following equivalent valuation formulas:

$$i = c \sum_{k=1}^{\tau} (1 + \rho')^{-k} + v(1 + \rho')^{-\tau}, \tag{4.8}$$

$$= c/\rho' + [v - (c/\rho')] (1 + \rho')^{-\tau}. \tag{4.9}$$

An illustration of Equation 4.8 was given in Chapter 2 for a coupon rate of 6 percent a year, a redemption value of 102 percent, a maturity of 7 years, and a discount rate ρ' equal to 12 percent a year. The investment value of such a bond turned out to be 73.52 percent of its nominal value.

It should be noted here that the investment value determined by Equations 4.4, 4.5, 4.8, and 4.9 represents the value of the straight bond features of the convertible bond, *inclusive of accrued interest*. Futhermore, these formulas only provide accurate investment values at the beginning of a coupon period, that is, *for integer values of τ*. Between two coupon payments, the investment value follows a time path that is different from the path described by these formulas. It can easily be shown that this time path is generated by a continuous growth of the investment value at a rate $\rho = \ln(1 + \rho')$ per coupon period. Each time a coupon is paid, the investment value i then suddenly drops by the coupon value c as a fraction of the nominal bond value. A more complete description of the time path of the investment value, that also applies to noninteger values of τ, is provided by Equation 4.31 for $\tau = t$ and for an accrual period with duration α. This formula is to be used in most practical applications, as the maturity of existing bonds is typically not equal to an integer number of coupon periods. For the time being, however, we will analyze the properties of the investment value assuming a maturity equal to an integer number of coupon periods. As these properties can easily be explained on intuitive grounds, we will present them below without mathematical proof.

The most elementary properties of the investment value can be described as follows. All other things being equal,

1. *the higher the coupon rate, the greater the investment value*;
2. *the greater the redemption value, the greater the investment value*;

3. *the higher the discount rate, the smaller the investment value*;

4. *if the discount rate* ρ' *is higher (lower) than the coupon rate* c', *then the investment value is smaller (greater) than the redemption value*;

5. *the less time to maturity, the greater (smaller) the investment value if the discount rate* ρ' *is higher (lower) than the coupon rate* c'.

These properties are in fact intuitively easy to explain. To start with, the higher the coupon rate, the higher the coupon payments and their present value, which obviously adds to the investment value. Second, a greater redemption value leads to a greater cash flow at the expiration date, which obviously causes the investment value to be greater as well. Third, the higher the discount rate, the smaller the present value of all principal and coupon payments, and therefore also the smaller the investment value. Fourth, if the bond is to be equally attractive as an investment vehicle as bonds currently issued at par, it has to sell below (above) par if the coupon rate on those new issues, which corresponds the current discount rate ρ', is above (below) the coupon rate c' of the existing bond in question. Fifth, as long as the same discount rate is considered, the investment value has to tend over time to its value at maturity, or its redemption value. This means that it will decrease over time whenever the current investment value is greater than its redemption value (when $\rho' < c'$), and that it will increase over time whenever its current investment value is smaller than its redemption value (when $c' < \rho'$).

The last three properties are illustrated in Figure 4.1, in which each curve represents the investment value of a given convertible bond at a constant discount rate over the remaining life of the bond. The higher the constant discount rate, the lower the corresponding curve. Each curve intersects the

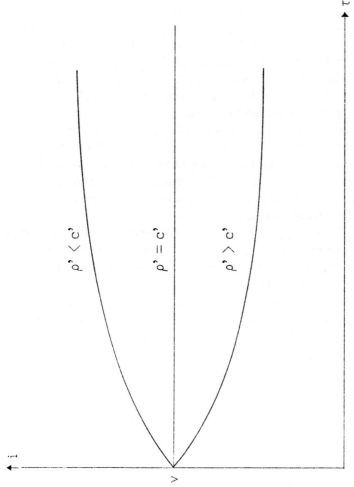

Figure 4.1

vertical axis at a level equal to the redemption value v, which corresponds to the fact that at the time of maturity (when $\tau = 0$), the investment value always coincides with the redemption value. The curve above the horizontal line represents the investment value of the bond at a discount rate ρ' that is smaller than the coupon rate c'. As this curve has a positive slope, the investment value declines over time as long as the discount rate does not change. The curve below the horizontal line, on the other hand, represents the investment value of the bond for a discount rate ρ' that is greater than c'. Its negative slope indicates that this investment value increases over time. The curve for which $\rho' = c'$ coincides with the horizontal line itself, which means that, if the discount rate is constantly equal to the coupon rate, the investment value will invariably be equal to the redemption value. As pointed out above, *these curves only represent correct investment values for integer values of τ.*

Other properties relate to the sensitivity of the investment value to changes in the discount rate. This sensitivity is usually measured by the *interest elasticity of the investment value,* which can be defined as *the relative change in the investment value as a fraction of the underlying relative change in the discount rate.* Depending on whether interest is compounded once per coupon period or continuously, this interest elasticity will be represented by $e^i_{\rho'}$ or e^i_ρ, respectively. It can be shown that

$$e^i_{\rho'} = -\frac{\rho'}{1+\rho'}d, \qquad (4.10)$$

and

$$e^i_\rho = -\rho d, \qquad (4.11)$$

where the minus signs just reflect the fact that the investment value and the discount rate always move in opposite directions,

and where *d* represents the *duration* of the bond. Both relationships express that *the interest elasticity of the investment
value is proportional to the duration*, and show a proportionality factor that is exclusively dependent on the discount
rate. The concept of "duration" must be distinguished from
the bond's remaining life or time to maturity, which by
definition corresponds to the *maximum* length of time that a
dollar can remain invested in the bond before flowing back to
the bondholder as part of a cash payment. In other words,
the bond's remaining life coincides with the maturity of the
last cash payment. The duration, on the other hand, is the
weighted average maturity of the whole stream of cash
payments, *with weights equal to the present values of these
cash payments as a fraction of the investment value*. As, by
definition, the investment value equals the sum of all these
present values, the weights add up to 1 as they should. A
coupon-bearing bond can be thought of as a portfolio of as
many zero coupon bonds as there are cash payments, such
that the *k*th zero coupon has an investment value equal to the
present value of the *k*th cash payment, and a maturity equal
to *k* coupon periods. The duration, then, is nothing more
than the weighted average maturity of this portfolio, with
weights equal to investment values of the zero coupon bonds
as a fraction of the investment value of the total portfolio.

   This can more precisely be expressed in mathematical terms
by rewriting Equation 4.8 in the following way:

$$(c/i) \sum_{k=1}^{\tau-1} (1 + \rho')^{-k} + [(v + c)/i](1 + \rho')^{-\tau} = 1 \qquad (4.12)$$

Each of the τ terms in the left-hand side of Equation 4.12
represents one of the weights used in the determination of the
duration. The first $\tau - 1$ terms are present values of the first
$\tau - 1$ coupon payments as a fraction of the investment

values, while the last term is the present value of the redemption payment and the accompanying payment of the last coupon, again as a fraction of the investment value. The duration, therefore, can be figured out by multiplying each of these weights by their corresponding maturity, and adding up these products over all cash payments. More specifically, the kth term in the left-hand side of Equation 4.12 is to be multiplied by k, for all k, and then all τ products obtained this way are to be added. This results in the following duration formulas:

$$d = (c/i) \sum_{k=1}^{\tau-1} k(1 + \rho')^{-k} + [(v + c)\tau/i](1 + \rho')^{-\tau} \quad (4.13)$$

$$= (c/i) \sum_{k=1}^{\tau} k(1 + \rho')^{-k} + (v\tau/i)(1 + \rho')^{-\tau} \quad (4.14)$$

In the case of continuous compounding at a rate ρ, the duration can equivalently be defined as follows:

$$d = (c/i) \sum_{k=1}^{\tau} ke^{-\rho k} + (v\tau/i)\, e^{-\rho\tau} \quad (4.15)$$

To illustrate this concept of duration, let us consider the example of Chapter 2 again. If we replace the different parameters in Equation 4.14 by the values taken by them in this example, we obtain the following numerical result:

$$d = (.06/.7352) \sum_{k=1}^{7} k(1.12)^{-k} + 7(1.02/.7352)\,(1.12)^{-7}$$

$$= 5.7158.$$

The duration of the bond therefore is 5 years and 71.58 percent of a year, or approximately 5 years and 261 days. Note that this duration is smaller than the bond's maturity of 7 years. Generally speaking, the duration never exceeds the maturity, and only coincides with the maturity in the case of a zero coupon bond. In fact, no simple relationship exists between the duration and the maturity of a coupon-bearing bond. In some cases a longer maturity may even result in a shorter duration. In view of Equation 4.10, the interest elasticity in this example equals $-$ (5.7158)(.12)/(1.12) $=$ $-$.6124.

The property according to which the sensitivity of the investment value, as measured by its interest elasticity, is proportional to the bond's duration, can easily be explained by intuitive reasoning. If the rate of interest decreases, for example, the investment value of any convertible bond will increase as it becomes more attractive to investors relative to new issues, which have a lower yield. By investing in the existing bond at the old price, investors can lock in the higher-than-current yield for a period of time equal to the maturity of the bond. However, to the degree that there are coupon payments before maturity, the total amount of money that is invested in this relatively high-yielding bond will suddenly drop by the value of a coupon whenever such a coupon is cashed by the bondholder. In view thereof, some dollars will remain invested in a coupon-bearing bond for a longer period of time than others, up to a maximum equal to the bond's maturity. As explained above, the average length of time during which these dollars remain invested, while earning a higher-than-current yield, equals the duration of the bond. As it can be expected that the relative increase in the investment value is proportional to the average length of time during which these higher yields can be locked in, it should be no surprise that the interest elasticity of the investment value is proportional to the duration of the bond.

The concept of duration was introduced by Macaulay (1938), but its relationship with the sensitivity of straight bond values to interest rate fluctuations was discovered by Fisher and Weil (1971), who revived the use of this concept and generalized it by allowing for variable rates of interest. The concept of duration also plays an important role in strategies that have been developed to "immunize" the value of a portfolio of straight coupon-bearing bonds against interest rate fluctuations. It can be shown that, all other things being equal, the duration will be longer, the lower the coupon rate, the larger the redemption value, and the lower the discount rate. Generally speaking, it is also true that a longer maturity will result in a longer duration, except for sufficiently large maturities in case the investment value is smaller than the par value.

Ignoring the conversion features of a convertible bond, some selection rules may be derived from the properties of the investment value described in this subsection. Strictly speaking, these rules only apply to straight bonds, but the underlying principle also plays a role in the selection of convertible bonds. Let us first consider expectations of a substantial rise in rates of interest over a relatively short period of time. We know that rising interest rates have a negative impact on investment values. All other things equal, therefore, *investors behave in a way that is consistent with these expectations, if they do not buy any straight bonds, or even sell off at least part of their bond portfolio to reduce the risk of a decrease in the portfolio's value. The bonds to be sold are the ones with the longest duration*, as the sensitivity of the bond's investment value to any change in the discount rate is proportional to its duration. The proportionality factor itself, which only depends on the discount rate, does not play any role in the selection process as long as the same discount rate is applied to all bonds under consideration. This can only be justified if they all belong to the same risk class. To the degree that they do not, the proportionality factor must be considered as well; that is, the absolute value of the interest elasticity rather than the duration should be used as a selection criterion. This principle also applies in those cases in which interest rates are expected to decline or in which there is a lot of uncertainty about their future course.

A policy that is consistent with expectations of declining interest rates calls for not selling any straight bonds, and even acquiring additional bonds at the current prices before they start rising in response to declining interest rates. Furthermore, in order to profit from such a purchase to a maximum degree, one should select bonds with the longest possible duration.

To the degree that one is uncertain about the future course of interest rates, *the corresponding interest risk can be reduced by selling straight bonds with a long duration and by holding or buying those with a relatively short duration.* Independent of the direction in which interest rates change, the impact of such a change on the value of one's bond portfolio would be relatively small.

For the sake of completeness, it should be mentioned that these rules are exclusively based on *interest effects*, the impact of changing interest rates on the investment value. They do *not* take into account any *time effect,* which refers to the impact on the investment value of a decreasing maturity when time goes by. This time effect will be discussed in more detail later in this chapter ("Properties of Bond Values and Derivation of Expected Bond Returns"), where the impact of the passage of time on the bond value as a whole is analyzed.

Although, strictly speaking, the above principles only apply to straight bonds, *they also apply to convertible bonds to the degree in which any impact from a change in interest rates on their investment value is not offset by an opposite impact on their option value.* We will indeed show later in this chapter that option and investment values move in opposite directions in response to any given change in interest rates.

Finally, it should also be pointed out as a practical matter that data on the duration and on the interest elasticity of bonds may not be readily available, and that it may be necessary to derive them from the four basic parameters c, v,

ρ, and τ for all bonds considered. As shown in the above example, this can easily be done with a relatively simple hand calculator, or even faster by means of a suitable computer program.

Basic properties of the option value

Let us now turn to the conversion side of a convertible bond. As the option value o of a convertible bond is represented by the second term of the right-hand side in Equation 4.1, we have the following relationship:

$$o = f(b_c + m, i_m + m, \sigma, r, t). \tag{4.16}$$

In view of Equation 4.2 it is clear that the investment value at maturity i_m depends on the same parameters as the current investment value, in addition to the time to maturity t of the conversion option. If we again let the unit of time coincide with the duration of a coupon period, and if we assume that both τ and t represent an integer number of coupon periods, the investment value at maturity is determined by the following equalities:

$$i_m = c \sum_{k=1}^{\tau-t} e^{-\rho k} + v e^{-\rho(\tau-t)}, \tag{4.17}$$

$$= \frac{c}{e^{\rho} - 1} + \left[v - \frac{c}{e^{\rho} - 1} \right] e^{-\rho(\tau-t)}. \tag{4.18}$$

From Equation 4.18 it is easily seen that i_m coincides with the redemption value v whenever $\tau = t$ (whenever the conversion option expires at the bond's maturity date). As this is generally the case, we can safely introduce this simplifying assumption into our analysis without unduly restricting the applicability of the model. Under this assumption, the exercise price of the conversion option would simply become equal to $v + m$, which means that it would no longer be dependent on c, ρ, τ, and t. Consequently, Equation 4.16 could be reduced to:

$$o = f(b_c + m, v + m, \sigma, r, t). \qquad (4.19)$$

If we introduce parameters $b_c{}'$ and $v\,'$, defined by

$$b_c{}' = b_c + m \qquad (4.20)$$

and

$$v\,' = v + m \qquad (4.21)$$

then Equation 4.19 can equivalently be written as:

$$o = f(b_c{}', v\,', \sigma, r, t). \qquad (4.22)$$

We will further rely in this section on the Black-Scholes specification of the value function f, to derive some basic properties of the option value and corresponding rules for convertible bond selection. This specification was described in Equations 3.47, 3.48, and 3.49 in Chapter 3. We will again omit all mathematical proofs of these properties, to leave more room for intuitive explanations and a discussion of their implications. Besides, most of these mathematical proofs are quite complicated, even when the properties themselves can easily be explained on intuitive grounds. Let us first consider a few of the more elementary properties. It can be shown that, all other things being equal, *the option value is greater,*

1. *the greater the stock price,*
2. *the smaller the redemption value,*
3. *the smaller the margin payments due by the bondholder,*
4. *the greater the volatility of the underlying stock,*
5. *the higher the risk-free rate of interest, and*
6. *the longer the time to maturity.*

The first of these properties is obvious, as the shares of common stock, for which the convertible bond can be exchanged, have a higher value if the share price is higher. Properties (2) and (3) can easily be understood as well, as the conversion option clearly has more value if its exercise price $v + m$ is smaller, either because the redemption value v is smaller, or because the margin payment m is smaller. Furthermore, since the upward potential of the option value in response to changes in the share price is greater than its downward potential, greater volatility of the underlying stock actually increases the value of the conversion option.

The fifth property is less obvious, but can be understood by referring to fully hedged positions that arbitrageurs can take by making *opposite* transactions in the stock market and in the call option market, determined by the *hedge ratio*. If the value of the options over the value of the stock shares equals this particular ratio, a risk-free portfolio of opposite positions in stocks and options is obtained, as changes in the value of the stock shares in this position are exactly offset by opposite changes in the value of the options on that stock. This hedge ratio can be shown to equal $\Phi(d_1)$ in Equation 3.11 of the Black-Scholes model, and is therefore smaller than 1. This means that the value of the options in a hedged position is always smaller than the value of the stock shares in that position. Therefore, any hedged position obtained by selling stock and buying options on the stock generates a positive cash flow, that can be invested at the risk-free rate of interest r. The higher this rate, the more attractive this kind of hedged position. The higher demand for options resulting from this will push their price upward. Similarly, arbitrageurs need to borrow money at the risk-free rate r to finance the negative cash flow generated by hedged positions of the opposite type (hedged positions that result from buying stock and writing options). The higher r is, the more expensive and the less attractive such a position. This in turn will lead arbitrageurs to write fewer options. The lower supply of options resulting from this will again push option prices upward. Summing up, call option values will move in the same direction as the risk-free rate of interest. And since conversion options are but a special case of call options, a similar conclusion can also be drawn with respect to option values of convertible bonds.

Finally, the sixth property expresses that the more time a bondholder has to exercise the conversion option, the more valuable that option is to him. More time indeed offers him more alternatives as to when the conversion option can be exercised, and more alternatives can only make the conversion option more attractive.

Next let us determine the sensitivity of the option value to changes in the stock price and in the rate of interest. The starting point for sensitivity analysis is the Black-Scholes valuation formula again:

$$o = b_c' \Phi(d_1) - v'e^{-rt} \Phi(d_2). \tag{4.23}$$

If we denote the first and the second term on the right side by o_1 and o_2, respectively, this valuation formula can also be written as:

$$o = o_1 - o_2, \tag{4.24}$$

where

$$o_1 = b_c' \Phi(d_1) \tag{4.25}$$

and

$$o_2 = v'e^{-rt} \Phi(d_2). \tag{4.26}$$

It can be shown that the *stock price elasticity* e_s^o of the option value, which measures the sensitivity of the option value to stock price changes and which is defined as *the relative change in the option value as a fraction of the underlying relative change in the stock price,* can be expressed as follows:

$$e_s^o = \frac{o_1}{o} . \tag{4.27}$$

Similarly, it can also be shown that the *interest elasticity e_r^o of the option value,* which measures the sensitivity of the option value to changes in the rate of interest r and which is defined as *the relative change of the option value as a fraction of the underlying relative change in the rate of interest,* is determined by the following formula:

$$e_r^o = rt \frac{o_2}{o} \tag{4.28}$$

In the example of Chapter 3 ("A Numerical Example"), the values of o, o_1, and o_2 turn out to be as follows:

$$o_1 = (1.071)(.8655) = .9270,$$

$$o_2 = (.4968) e^{-(.07)(7.75)} = .2888,$$

$$o = .9270 - .2888 = .6382,$$

for an interest rate r of 7 percent per year and a remaining option life of 7.75 years. By substituting these values in Equations 4.27 and 4.28, the following elasticities are found:

$$e_s^o = .9270/.6382 = 1.4525,$$

$$e_r^o = (.07)(7.75)(.2888)/.6382 = .2455.$$

Since $e_s^o > 1$ in this example, *the option value of the convertible bond under consideration will react more than proportionately to changes in the stock price* and, since $e_r^o < 1$, *it will react less than proportionately to changes in the rate of interest*. This is also the way in which option values of convertible bonds behave in general.

The relative magnitudes of these two elasticities of the option value, as well as the relative magnitudes of the expected changes in the underlying stock prices and in the risk-free rate of interest, play an important role in the determination of the expected bond returns. Obviously, the expected change in the option value of a convertible bond not only depends on the sensitivity of that option value to changes in the underlying stock price, but also on the magnitude of those changes. As different stock prices can generally be expected to change in different degrees, more sensitive option values need not necessarily change by a greater percentage. They can indeed change by a smaller percentage if their underlying stock price changes by a smaller percentage. We will therefore also take into account any differences among expected price changes of underlying stocks when comparing different convertible bonds.

If convertible bonds are to be selected not only on the basis of their expected return, but also on the basis of risk considerations, one should not restrict the analysis to point estimates of future changes in stock prices and interest rates. In theory, one should consider all possible degrees of change and assign appropriate probabilities to them that reflect the investor's degree of belief in their occurrence. This means that joint probability distributions should be defined for changes in both stock prices and interest rates. Next, one should derive the corresponding probability distributions for the return on each feasible portfolio of convertible bonds. Finally, the portfolio with the best probability distribution for its return—or, in simplified version, the best risk–expected return combination—should be selected. The procedure of selecting a unique optimal portfolio could be formalized by specifying a utility function over the different alternative probability distributions or risk–expected return combinations, and by selecting the alternative with the maximum utility. This theoretical scheme, however, will not be adopted in this text, as it is very difficult to apply in view of the many parameters that need to be estimated, and in view of the complexity of the calculations. We will, instead, confine ourselves to a brief outline of the way in which risk can be taken into account within the framework of Markowitz's portfolio model at the end of this chapter.

PROPERTIES OF BOND VALUES AND DERIVATION OF EXPECTED BOND RETURNS

As we plan to rank convertible bonds in order of decreasing expected returns, we will focus in this section on the derivation of these returns from the expected return on the stock market as a whole, and from the expected rate of change of interest rates. To show how these expected bond returns can be derived in practical applications, let us consider an example of 10 different convertible bonds with only one common feature, namely the length of the time between two coupon payments or, in other words, the duration of their coupon periods. Although the analysis of this section can easily be extended to include convertible bonds that feature coupon payments at different time intervals, we simply assume for the sake of convenience that all bonds have coupon periods of, say, half a year. This means that the bondholder is entitled to two coupon payments equal to half the annual coupon rate times the nominal bond value. Furthermore, we also assume that the conversion option of each bond expires at the maturity date of that bond (i.e., we also assume that the time to maturity τ of any given bond is equal to the time to maturity t of its conversion option). Both maturities will be expressed in semesters and denoted by one and the same symbol, t. The annually compounded riskless rate of interest is supposed to take a value of 7 1/4 percent per year. The equivalent continuously compounded rate of interest is therefore equal to ln 1.0725 $\simeq$ 7 percent per year. The corresponding semi-annual rates r' and r therefore equal half these annual percentages, or 3 5/8 percent and approximately 3 1/2 percent, respectively. As the bonds generally have different maturities and belong to different risk-classes, we must apply different discount rates to determine their investment value. The semiannually compounded discount rates per semester are supposed to equal half the annual percentages in column 5 of Table 4.1, and are denoted by ρ' in Equations 4.8 and 4.9. In practice, they are to be derived from the yield curves for the different risk-classes involved. Similarly, the semiannual coupon payment c corresponds to half the annual percentages of the nominal bond value given in column 2. Column 1 simply contains the numerical order of the bonds considered, while columns 3 and 4 represent their redemption value and maturity, respectively. This way, all relevant straight bond characteristics of the 10 convertible bonds analyzed in this numerical example are shown in columns 2 through 5.

On the other hand, the values of the parameters that affect the option value of the bond (the conversion price p_c, the required side payment m, and the stock price S) are given in columns 6, 7, and 8.

Although the volatility of the bonds also affects their option value, it will not be treated as an exogenous parameter. To approximate reality as closely as possible, we will, on the contrary, derive the volatility of each bond from its current price. The current bond prices, *exclusive* of accrued interest, are given in column 9. For each bond, we determined the value of the volatility of its underlying stock in such a way that there is

Table 4.1

#	2c(%)	v(%)	t(sem)	2ρ'(%)	p_c(\$)	m(%)	S(\$)	price(%)
1	5	100	29.15	9.21	41	0	$45^{1/2}$	142
2	9	102	24	9.03	$28^{1/2}$	0	19	$137^{3/8}$
3	$7^{5/8}$	100	32.64	9.26	59	18	$89^{3/8}$	$204^{1/4}$
4	11	101	13.12	8.86	95	0	123	$189^{3/8}$
5	$6^{1/4}$	100	23.36	9.02	$48^{1/4}$	0	$22^{7/8}$	116
6	$3^{1/4}$	103	4.45	8.68	78	$14^{3/4}$	$46^{1/8}$	$95^{5/8}$
7	$10^{3/8}$	100	28.31	9.17	$43^{3/4}$	0	$109^{1/2}$	348
8	$4^{5/8}$	100	9.79	8.80	55	0	51	$113^{3/8}$
9	6	$99^{1/2}$	14	8.89	$77^{1/2}$	10	33	$103^{1/2}$
10	5	100	17.16	8.93	120	0	33	$89^{7/8}$

no disparity between (1) the theoretical bond value implied by the Black-Scholes valuation formula and (2) the actual current bond price *inclusive* of any accrued interest. This method provides us with an estimate of the volatility that is consistent with the market price of each bond. To the degree that the bond market values all convertible bonds in an efficient way, such an estimate should be very reliable. At the same time, this method of determining the volatility is simpler than its direct estimation on the basis of historical data. It only takes a few trials, or a suitable computer program, to find the σ-value that corresponds to a given bond price. One should begin by making an educated guess at this σ-value, and by figuring the corresponding option value o by means of the Black-Scholes formula. This option value is then added to the investment value i to obtain the bond value b. By subtracting from b the accrued interest a, the bond price (exclusive of accrued interest) is obtained that corresponds to the guessed σ-value. If this price is greater (smaller) than the quoted current price, one repeats the same procedure with a smaller (greater) σ-value. Obviously, the difference between the new and old σ-values should be somewhat in proportion to the disparity between the calculated bond price and the quoted bond price. By just a few repetitive iterations, it is possible this way to gradually approximate the σ-value that corresponds to the quoted price. The process can obviously be speeded up considerably by using a suitable computer program or spreadsheet template. The σ-values of the 10 convertible bonds under consideration, that are shown in column 6 of Table 4.2, were actually determined by means of a spreadsheet template. Once the σ-values are found for all bonds, they can be used to derive the elasticities of the option values shown in Table 4.3

Note that the coupon value, the redemption value, the margin payment, and the bond price are expressed in Table 4.1 as a percentage of the nominal bond value, while the conversion price and the stock price are expressed in dollar terms. As usual, the discount rate is shown as an annual percentage. Finally, the remaining life of the bond in column 4 is expressed in terms of semesters rather than years, in view of the fact that coupon payments are made semiannually.

In addition to the volatility, we can also derive other characteristics of the conversion option, as for example, the conversion value b_c and the factors o_1 and o_2 used in the determination of the option value o. The values of all these option characteristics show up in columns 5, 7, 8, and 9 of Table 4.2.

Columns 2 to 4, on the other hand, represent straight bond characteristics, namely the accrued interest a, the investment value (inclusive of the accrued interest) i, and the bond duration

Table 4.2

#	a(%)	i(%)	d(sem)	b_c(%)	σ	o_1(%)	o_2(%)	o(%)
1	2.13	68.71	18.34	110.98	.16073	109.18	33.76	75.41
2	0.00	100.48	15.20	66.67	.33472	55.05	18.15	36.90
3	1.37	87.73	17.87	133.48	.28058	145.98	28.08	117.90
4	4.84	115.87	9.47	129.47	.40189	114.63	36.28	78.34
5	2.00	82.23	15.68	47.41	.66679	41.68	5.91	35.77
6	0.89	92.59	4.28	44.38	.37817	15.00	11.08	3.93
7	3.58	113.00	15.50	250.29	.78650	246.08	7.50	238.58
8	0.49	84.16	8.72	92.73	.23401	72.40	42.70	29.70
9	0.00	84.90	11.39	32.58	.56118	28.47	9.87	18.60
10	2.10	78.88	13.29	27.50	.59294	18.73	5.64	13.09

d in semesters. Except for the duration and the square root of the volatility, all parameter values in Table 4.2 are expressed as a percentage of the nominal bond value.

While we already explained how the σ-values in column 6 were obtained, columns 7 to 9 need no further clarification, as the figures in these columns are simply derived from the data in Table 4.1, from the volatility, and from the conversion value, by means of the Black-Scholes valuation formula. The conversion values of column 5 were derived from the stock price, the conversion price, and the margin payment according to the following formula:

$$b_c = \frac{S}{p_c} - m. \qquad (4.29)$$

Table 4.3

#	b(%)	i/b	o/b	e^i_ρ	e^o_r	e^o_s	e^b_r	e^b_s
1	144.13	0.48	0.52	−0.83	0.46	1.45	−0.15	0.76
2	137.38	0.73	0.27	−0.67	0.41	1.49	−0.38	0.40
3	205.62	0.43	0.57	−0.81	0.27	1.24	−0.19	0.71
4	194.21	0.60	0.40	−0.41	0.21	1.46	−0.16	0.59
5	118.00	0.70	0.30	−0.69	0.14	1.17·	−0.44	0.35
6	96.52	0.96	0.04	−0.18	0.44	3.82	−0.16	0.16
7	351.58	0.32	0.68	−0.69	0.03	1.03	−0.20	0.70
8	113.86	0.74	0.26	−0.38	0.49	2.44	−0.15	0.64
9	103.50	0.82	0.18	−0.50	0.26	1.53	−0.36	0.28
10	91.97	0.86	0.14	−0.58	0.26	1.43	−0.46	0.20

Although this formula is accurate only if the ratio of the nominal value of the converted bonds over the conversion price is an integer, it allows us to come up with an approximate value that is close enough to the true conversion value for the purpose of this numerical illustration. The exact conversion value depends on the applicable fraction rule, and can be figured out by following the procedure described in Chapter 2 (under "Determining the Conversion Value").

The accrued interest, on the other hand, is determined by the following formula:

$$a = \alpha c, \qquad (4.30)$$

where α stands for the fraction of the current coupon period that has already elapsed. In the present illustration, for example, $\alpha = 1 - .15 = .85$ for the first bond, as $t = 29.15$.

The formula underlying the investment values of column 3 is in fact different from Equation 4.9, considered earlier in this chapter. The reason is that Equation 4.9 was based on the assumption that the current date coincides with the beginning of a coupon period, while this is generally not the case for the bonds considered in the present illustration. The more general formula used in Table 4.2 looks as follows:

$$i = (c/\rho\,')\,(1 + \rho\,')^{\alpha} + [v - (c/\rho\,')](1 + \rho\,')^{-t}. \qquad (4.31)$$

If the current date happens to coincide with the coupon date for any given bond, α would take a zero value, and Equation 4.31 would clearly be reduced to Equation 4.9.

Finally, the only remaining unexplained column of Table 4.2 is the duration column. The starting point for deriving the values of this column is Equation 4.14. This formula, however, was also based on the assumption that the current date is a coupon date. The required adjustment can easily be made by first determining an approximate duration by setting α equal to zero. This comes down to applying Equation 4.14 for a time to maturity that results from rounding t to the nearest greater integer. Then subtract α from this approximation to find the correct duration of the bond under consideration.

It can be quite time-consuming, however, to apply Equation 4.14 if there are many coupon payments to consider. The reason is that the use of this formula requires the summation of as many terms as there are coupon payments. To avoid a lengthy calculation time, it is recommended to use the following simpler duration formula instead:

$$d = t + [1 - (v/i)(1 + \rho\,')^{-t} - (c/i)(t + \alpha)(1 + \rho\,')^{-(1-\alpha)}]$$
$$\frac{1 + \rho\,'}{\rho\,'}. \qquad (4.32)$$

This formula also takes into account the fraction α of the current coupon period that passed. For $\alpha = 0$ we obtain a formula that is equivalent to Equation 4.14.

Note that t denotes the maturity in coupon periods in Equations 4.31 and 4.32, while c represents a single coupon payment as a fraction of the nominal bond value. The variable ρ' represents the discount rate per coupon period, assuming that interest is compounded once per coupon period.

Let us next turn to Table 4.3, which focuses on the elasticities of the investment value, the option value, and the bond value. As explained in previous sections, these elasticities measure the sensitivity of those values to changes in the rates of interest and in the underlying stock price. The most important of these elasticities, namely the elasticities of the bond values, play an important role in the determination of the bond returns for any given expectations about the future course of interest rates and the stock market as a whole.

The bond values themselves are represented as a percentage of the nominal value in the second column, and are simply obtained by adding the investment and option values that appear in Table 4.2. The figures in columns 3 and 4 indicate which fraction of the bond value results from the straight bond characteristics of the convertible bond, and which fraction is due to its conversion option. These fractions are the weights by which investment and option elasticities must be multiplied to obtain the corresponding elasticities of the bond values, as shown in Equations 4.33 and 4.34:

$$e_s^b = (i/b)\, e_s^i + (o/b)\, e_s^o, \tag{4.33}$$

$$e_r^b = (i/b)\, e_r^i + (o/b)\, e_r^o. \tag{4.34}$$

Since the investment value is independent of the stock price, it is insensitive to changes in that price (that is, $e_s^i = 0$). Equation 4.33 can therefore be reduced to:

$$e_s^b = (o/b) \, e_s^o. \qquad (4.35)$$

On the other hand, the investment value is only dependent on changes in the risk-free rate of interest r, to the degree that they induce any change in the discount rate ρ that applies to the bond's risk class. Normally, r and ρ will fluctuate in the same direction. In general, the following relationship can be shown to exist:

$$e_r^i = e_\rho^i e_r^\rho, \qquad (4.36)$$

where e_r^ρ represents the elasticity of ρ relative to changes in r. When substituting the right side of this equality for e_r^i in Equation 4.34, we obtain:

$$e_r^b = (i/b) \, e_\rho^i e_r^\rho + (o/b) \, e_r^o. \qquad (4.37)$$

If there is reason to believe that the discount rate ρ and the risk-free rate r fluctuate in about the same relative proportions, one could safely assume that $e_r^\rho = 1$, and Equation 4.37 could be simplified to

$$e_r^b = (i/b) \, e_\rho^i + (o/b) \, e_r^o. \qquad (4.38)$$

If not, a suitable value of e_r^ρ should be estimated from historical data and substituted on the right side of Equation 4.37.

The interest and stock price elasticities e_r^b and e_s^b of the bond value, that are shown in columns 8 and 9 of Table 4.3, are derived from the corresponding elasticities of the investment and option values according to Equations 4.38 and 4.35, respectively. The interest and stock price elasticities e_r^o and e_s^o of the option value shown in columns 6 and 7 are determined by Equations 4.27 and 4.28, while the interest elasticities e_p^i of the investment value shown in column 5, are derived from Equation 4.11.

It can be seen from Table 4.3 that a typical convertible bond has the following properties:

1. Investment and option values have a negative and a positive interest elasticity, respectively. In absolute value, these interest elasticities are smaller than 1, but in most cases the interest elasticity of the investment value is greater in absolute value than the interest elasticity of the option value. That is, *a sudden change in interest rates causes the investment value to change in the opposite direction and induces a change in the option value in the same direction. In addition, it affects both the investment value and the option value less than proportionately, but in most cases it affects the investment value more than the option value.*

2. The interest elasticities of the investment and bond values are negative and smaller than 1 in absolute value, but the interest elasticity of the investment value exceeds in absolute value the interest elasticity of the bond value; that is, *a sudden change in interest rates has an opposite and less than proportionate impact on both the investment value and the bond value, but the impact on the investment value is larger than on the bond value.*

3. The stock price elasticities of the option and bond values are positive, but they are greater than 1 for the option value and smaller than 1 for the bond value; that is, *a sudden change in the price of the underlying stock causes both the option value and the bond value to change in the same direction as the stock price itself, but affects the option value more than proportionately and the bond value less than proportionately.*

These findings imply the following important properties of convertible bonds:

a. *A convertible bond is less vulnerable to a sudden rise in interest rates than a straight bond with the same coupon payments, coupon dates, redemption value, and maturity, but at the same time it is less profitable than such a straight bond when interest rates decline.*

b. *A convertible bond is less vulnerable to a sudden decline in the price of the underlying stock than the stock itself, but at the same time it is less profitable than the stock when its price rises.*

These properties mean in fact that convertible bond values fluctuate less in response to sudden changes in interest rates than corresponding straight bond values, and fluctuate less in response to sudden changes in the price of the underlying stock than the value of the stock itself. To that degree investments in convertible bonds could be considered less risky than both investments in corresponding straight bonds and investments in the underlying stock.

It should be noted that, strictly speaking, the changes in interest rate and stock price levels referred to in the above statements should occur instantaneously. That is why we used the attribute "sudden" to describe these changes. However, if we assume that the changes occur over a short period of time, these statements need no longer apply in all cases. For example, *statement (a) may no longer apply if interest rates increase.* This can easily be understood by reasoning as follows. All other things being equal, a small time elapse tends to increase the investment value at a rate equal to the discount rate ρ of the bond, and to decrease the option value at a rate equal to the risk-free rate of interest r. The corresponding change in the bond value, which is typically positive, will reflect both the increase in the investment value and the decrease in the option value. As a result, the passage of time causes the bond value to increase by a smaller percentage than the investment value. This time effect will therefore enlarge the difference in the percentage increases in the investment and the bond value caused by a decrease in interest rates. However, if interest rates increase, the time effect will completely or partially off-set the decrease in the investment and bond values that results from such an increase. This interference due to the passage of time may render statement (a) invalid in such a case, and in-vestment and bond values could even change in different directions.

Statements (a) and (b) also relate to isolated changes in in-terest rates and in the price of the underlying stock. If such changes are considered simultaneously and occur over a relatively small period of time, it can easily be shown that *the expected rate of return on the bond is a weighted average of the expected rate of return on the straight bond investment[1] and the expected rate of return on the conversion option,* in conformity with the following relationship:

$$R_b = (i/b) R_i + (o/b) R_o \qquad (4.39)$$

where R_b, R_i, and R_o represent the expected instantaneous an-nualized rates of return on the convertible bond as a whole, on the straight bond investment, and on the conversion op-tion, respectively. R_i can be shown to be related to the ex-pected instantaneous annualized rate of change R_ρ of the semiannual continuously compounded discount rate ρ in the following way:

$$R_i = e^i_\rho R_\rho + 2\rho. \qquad (4.40)$$

The first term in the right side represents the *interest effect*, the rate of change in the investment value caused by an in-stantaneous change in the discount rate ρ, while the second term represents the *time effect* or the rate of change in the in-vestment value resulting from the passage of time. The time effect takes into account that interest is accruing over time.

The time effect can be shown to coincide with the discount rate. Since the discount rate ρ is defined on a semiannual basis, the annualized time effect is obtained by doubling ρ. As this has no impact on the interest effect, the latter can be defined relative to ρ instead of to 2ρ. If we assume for convenience that ρ and r change in the same proportion and in the same direction, we have the following relationships:

$$e_r^i = e_\rho^i , \tag{4.41}$$

$$R_r = R_\rho, \tag{4.42}$$

where R_r stands for the expected instantaneous annualized rate of change of the continuously compounded risk-free rate of interest r. In view thereof, Equation 4.40 can also be written as:

$$R_i = e_r^i R_r + 2\rho, \tag{4.43}$$

which is equivalent to

$$R_i = 2\rho[1 - (d/2) R_r], \tag{4.44}$$

where 2ρ is the annualized discount rate and $d/2$ the duration of the bond in years.

Ignoring the impact of any stock dividend payments on the option value, it can also be shown that the instantaneous rate of return R_o on the conversion option can be split into different components as follows:

$$R_o = (o_1/o) R_{o_1} - (o_2/o) R_{o_2}, \tag{4.45}$$

$$= (o_1/o) R_S - (o_2/o) (2r)[1 - (t/2)R_r], \tag{4.46}$$

where R_{o_1}, R_{o_2}, and R_s represent the expected instantaneous annualized rates of change of o_1, o_2, and S, respectively.[2] The factor $2r[1 - (t/2)R_r]$ can be shown to be the expected instantaneous annualized return on a risk-free zero coupon bond with a maturity of $t/2$ years. By rearranging terms, Equation 4.46 can be rewritten as

$$R_o = (o_1/o)\,R_s + (rto_2/o)\,R_r - (o_2/o)(2r), \qquad (4.47)$$

which in view of Equations 4.27 and 4.28 is equivalent to

$$R_o = e_s^o\,R_s + e_r^o R_r - (2/t)\,e_r^o. \qquad (4.48)$$

The return on the conversion option can therefore be considered the cumulative result of three different effects, namely a *stock price effect*, which corresponds to the first term in these latter equations, an *interest effect*, which is represented by the second term, and a *time effect*, which is shown as the third term. These effects reflect the contributions to the option return from stock price changes, interest rate changes, and the passage of time, respectively.

These expressions for the expected rates of return on the straight bond investment and on the conversion option can next be substituted for R_i and R_o in Equation 4.39. The following results are obtained:

$$\mathbf{R}_b = (o/b)\,e_s^o R_s + [(i/b)\,e_r^i + (o/b)\,e_r^o]\,R_r$$
$$+ [2(\rho i - ro_2)/b], \qquad (4.49)$$

$$= e_s^b R_s + e_r^b R_r + [2(\rho i - ro_2)/b], \qquad (4.50)$$

$$= (o_1/b)\,R_s - [(d\rho i - tro_2)/b]\,R_r + [2(\rho i - ro_2)/b]. \qquad (4.51)$$

The first term on these right sides again represents the *stock price effect* on the bond value, the second term the *interest effect,* and the third term the *time effect*. All these effects reflect contributions from stock price changes, interest rate changes, and the passage of time to the expected bond return.

Alternatively, R_b can also be determined by means of the following relationship:

$$R_b = (i/b) R_i + (o_1/b) R_s - (o_2/b) (2r) [1 - (t/2)R_r]. \qquad (4.52)$$

Since $2r[1 - (t/2)R_r]$ is the instantaneous annualized rate of return on a risk-free zero coupon bond, this equation in fact tells us that the expected rate of return on the convertible bond equals the expected rate of return on a certain portfolio of straight bonds, underlying stock, and risk-free zero coupon bonds. The straight bonds have characteristics that are identical to the straight-bond characteristics of the convertible bond. The risk-free zero coupon bonds can be thought of as Treasury securities with a maturity equal to the remaining life of $t/2$ years of the conversion option. A fraction i/b of the total value of the portfolio must be invested in the straight bonds, a fraction equal to o_1/b must be invested in the underlying stock, while a fraction equal to $-o_2/b$ must be invested in the risk-free bonds. The negative sign of the last fraction in fact indicates that a short position has to be taken in those risk-free bonds. This means that the long positions in the straight bonds and in the underlying stock are to be partly financed by the proceeds from the short position. Since $(i/b) + (o_1/b) - (o_2/b) = (i + o_1 - o_2)/b = b/b = 1$, these fractions add up to 100 percent, as it should be. Obviously, they also change over time, which implies that the portfolio should, in principle, be reshuffled on a continuing basis if one wants it to remain equivalent to the convertible bond. The equivalent portfolio fractions for each of the 10 convertible bonds considered in our numerical illustration are shown in Table 4.4.

Before we can figure out the expected return on the 10 bonds of our numerical illustration, one last characteristic of those bonds must be introduced, namely the value of the so-called

Table 4.4

#	i/b(%)	o$_1$/b(%)	-o$_2$/b (%)
1	47.67	75.75	-23.43
2	73.14	40.07	-13.21
3	42.66	70.99	-13.66
4	59.66	59.02	-18.68
5	69.69	35.32	-5.01
6	95.93	15.54	-11.48
7	32.14	69.99	-2.13
8	73.91	63.58	-37.50
9	82.03	27.51	-9.54
10	85.76	20.37	-6.13

beta parameter of the stocks underlying these bonds. This parameter is named after the symbol β by which it is conventionally denoted in the *capital asset pricing model*. This well-known model, also referred to as the *Sharpe-Lintner model*, explains how capital assets in general, and stocks in particular, are priced in the capital markets. Usually the model is applied to just the stock market, and the β parameter of a stock represents the *systematic* or *nondiversifiable* risk associated with that stock as a fraction of the risk associated with the *market portfolio*,[3] that is, the portfolio of all outstanding shares of all traded stocks or any down-scaled version of it. This β factor measures the sensitivity of the stock price to upward and downward movements of the stock market as a whole. If the β-value of a stock is greater (smaller) than 1, its price tends to react more (less) than proportionately to fluctuations in the overall market. The price of any stock with a β-value equal to 1 tends to fluctuate in the same proportion as the value of the market portfolio. And the higher the β value of a stock, the more responsive the stock's price to upward or downward movements in the stock market as a whole. Estimates of the β-values of stocks are made available and are regularly updated by a number of financial service companies. The stocks underlying the 10 bonds in the numerical illustration of this section are supposed to have the β-values shown in column 2 of Table 4.5.

Table 4.5

#	β	R_s(%)	R_i(%)	R_o(%)	R_b(%)	stock price effect	interest effect	time effect	#
1	1.50	19.00	-18.49	39.58	11.90	14.39	-5.15	2.65	1
2	0.95	14.60	-13.52	32.10	-1.27	5.85	-12.65	5.54	8
3	1.14	16.12	-17.89	27.35	8.05	11.44	-6.30	2.91	4
4	1.22	16.76	-5.01	28.36	8.45	9.89	-5.30	3.87	3
5	1.13	16.04	-14.21	22.03	-3.22	5.67	-14.68	5.80	9
6	0.45	10.60	2.43	35.39	3.77	1.65	-5.22	7.35	6
7	1.78	21.24	-14.17	22.73	10.87	14.87	-6.73	2.73	2
8	0.86	13.88	-3.89	40.17	7.60	8.83	-4.96	3.74	5
9	1.20	16.60	-7.80	30.36	-0.94	4.57	-11.98	6.47	7
10	0.70	12.60	-10.59	23.62	-5.72	2.57	-15.35	7.06	10

The expected rates of return on the underlying stock in the third column are derived from these β-values and from an expected instantaneous annualized rate of return on the stock market portfolio of 15 percent, in conformity with the following fundamental relationship of the capital asset pricing model[4]:

$$R_s = 2r + \beta(R_m - 2r), \tag{4.53}$$

where R_m represents the expected instantaneous annualized rate of return on the market portfolio, and where $2r$ represents the continuously compounded annual risk-free rate of return. By substituting a value of 15 percent for R_m, a value of approximately 3.5 percent for r, and the values in the second column of Table 4.5 for β, values for R_s are obtained that are shown in the third column.

The expected rates of return R_i in column 4 are derived from Equation 4.43, assuming that the annually compounded risk-free rate of interest $2r'$ is expected to rise instantaneously at an annual rate of 250 basis points, or 2.5 percentage points. The corresponding instantaneous annualized rate of change of the continuously compounded risk-free rate of interest r can be shown to be equal to:

$$
\begin{aligned}
R_r &= \frac{\Delta(2r')/10,000}{(1 + 2r') \ln(1 + 2r')} \tag{4.54} \\
&= \frac{0.025}{1.0725 \ln 1.0725} = 33.3\%,
\end{aligned}
$$

where $\Delta(2r')$ represents the number of basis points by which $2r'$ changes on an annual basis. The values of R_i in column 4 can then be obtained by substituting this value of 33.3 percent for R_r in Equation 4.43, and using the values of e_r^i and ρ' from previous tables. Note that $R_i > 0$ for bond 6. In view of

128   *Convertible Bonds*

the fact that it has a maturity of only 4.45 semesters, the interest elasticity of its investment value shown in Table 4.3 is not more than 0.18 in absolute value. This, in turn, causes the interest effect on its investment value to be smaller than the time effect. All other bonds more typically have straight bond characteristics that lead to a negative return.

The values of R_o in column 5 are derived from Equations 4.47 or 4.48. Plugging the values of R_i and R_o into Equation 4.39 results in the expected bond returns R_b shown in column 6, while these bond returns have been split into three components in columns 7, 8, and 9, that correspond to the stock price effect, the interest effect, and the time effect, respectively.

Finally, all bonds are ranked in order of decreasing expected returns in column 10. Evidently, bond 1 is expected to give the highest annualized return of 11.9 percent, and is therefore ranked first. Bond 10, on the other hand, gets the worst score, with a negative expected rate of return of -5.72 percent. In total, six bonds turn out to have a positive expected return, while the remaining four are expected to yield a negative return. Such a negative return shows up whenever the negative interest effect outweighs the positive stock price and time effects. Bonds that are expected to decline in value should obviously be avoided.

More attractive current rates of return can be expected, if interest rates would decrease rather than increase, and if at the same time the return on the stock market as whole is expected to be greater. Thus, if the annually compounded risk-free rate of interest in the previous example is expected to decrease in a very short period of time at an annual rate of 150 basis points, and if the stock market as whole is expected to increase in that same period at an annual rate of 30 percent, current rates of return for the bonds can be expected that correspond to the figures in column 6 of Table 4.6. Using

Table 4.6

#	β	R_s (%)	R_i (%)	R_o (%)	R_b (%)	stock price effect	interest effect	time effect	#
1	1.50	41.50	25.50	47.82	37.18	31.44	3.09	2.65	2
2	0.95	28.85	22.24	31.34	24.69	11.56	7.59	5.54	6
3	1.14	33.22	25.22	34.03	30.27	23.58	3.78	2.91	3
4	1.22	35.06	16.88	43.81	27.74	20.69	3.18	3.87	4
5	1.13	32.99	22.64	34.59	26.26	11.65	8.81	5.80	5
6	0.45	17.35	12.13	37.77	13.18	2.70	3.13	7.35	10
7	1.78	47.94	22.85	48.61	40.33	33.55	4.04	2.73	1
8	0.86	26.78	16.11	45.37	23.75	17.03	2.98	3.74	7
9	1.20	34.60	18.60	44.06	23.17	9.52	7.19	6.47	8
10	0.70	23.10	20.33	24.86	20.98	4.70	9.21	7.06	9

Equation 4.54 again, one can verify that a decrease in $2r'$ by 150 basis points corresponds to a value of R_r equal to -19.98 percent.

Under these assumptions, the expected rates of return turn out to be positive for all bonds. It can be seen from the ranks in column 10 of that table that this time bond 7 would have the highest expected rate of return, namely 40.33 percent per year, while the winner in the previous example, bond 1, takes a second place. Also, bond 6 replaces bond 10 as the least promising bond. It is easily verified that no single bond has the same rank in both scenarios, illustrating the fact that the ranks generally depend on the specific expectations of the investor with respect to interest rates and stock prices.

DERIVATION OF EXPECTED PERIOD RETURNS OF CONVERTIBLE BONDS

The drawback of the method of the previous section is that it tells us only what the expected *instantaneous* bond returns are, given any expected *instantaneous* rates of change of interest rates and stock prices. In other words, the results only tell us which bonds are best *momentarily*. This would be no drawback at all in the absence of any transaction costs. If these costs were zero, one could reshuffle one's portfolio every day one or more times without any cost in terms of money and time. In such an ideal world, R_b would be a perfectly suitable selection criterion, apart from any risk considerations. However, in view of the substantial transaction costs incurred in reality, it is better not to reshuffle one's portfolio too frequently; that is, one should do it instead at sufficiently long time intervals. At the end of each interval one might determine bond ranks in the way illustrated above, and then reshuffle one's portfolio accordingly. There is, however, always a risk that bonds that start out growing fast in value end up growing slowly. Such bonds may therefore not respresent an optimal choice over such a time interval *as a whole*, even though they look very promising momentarily.

To avoid this kind of complication, one could try to determine bond ranks based on their profitability between the beginning and the end of such an interval. For example, a bond portfolio manager may want to determine which bonds can be expected to be most profitable over a time span of one month, based on her specific expectations about the behavior of interest rates and individual stock prices during that same month. In such a case, four parameters used in the valuation model of Chapter 3 will change in that month, namely S, r, ρ, and t. Given the manager's expected rates of change for interest rates and stock prices over that month, she can easily figure out the corresponding expected values of the first three parameters at the end of the month. For these parameter values, and for values of t that are one month less than its original values, she could then make a projection for the bond values at the end of the month. By adding the projected value of each bond to the value of any coupon payment during the month, and comparing this sum with the current bond value, she could finally determine the expected profitability of all bonds over the month, and assign ranks accordingly.

Obviously, the time interval of one month is completely arbitrary. In principle, it corresponds to the period of time during which no transactions are considered. As pointed out above, the interval should be long enough to avoid excessive transaction costs. At the same time, however, it should be short enough to allow the manager to adjust her portfolio fast enough in response to changing expectations, in order to ensure its optimality in a continuing way. In addition, it should be short enough to allow her to ignore the time value of any expiring coupons within the time span of the interval. Basically, the decision on the time interval must be made in a discretionary manner, and should reflect the specific concerns of the manager. In the following numerical illustration of how a bond's expected period return can be determined, we will again assume that an interval of one month has been selected.

Let us start out again with the same 10 bonds that we considered earlier in this section, and assume that the portfolio manager expects the annual risk-free rate of return $2r'$ to decrease over the month at an annual rate of 200 basis points. In addition, assume that she expects the value of the stock market portfolio to increase over that same period of a month at an annual rate of 35 percent. In the previous section, we assumed an expected instantaneous decrease in $2r'$ at an annual rate of 150 basis points and an expected instantaneous increase in the value of the market portfolio at an annual rate of 30 percent per year. As the expected period changes are greater than the corresponding expected instantaneous changes, interest rates and stock prices are in fact expected to change in an accelerated way within the time interval of a month.

Since the current value of the annually compounded risk-free rate of interest $2r'$ is 7.25 percent, the expected end-of-the-month value of $2r'$ is 7.25 percent $- (0.02/12) = 7.08$ percent. The corresponding value of the continuously compounded rate $2r$ equals ln $1.0708 = 6.84$ percent, which represents a decrease in the value of r of about 2.22 percent. As by assumption the continuously compounded discount rates ρ change in the same proportion as r, they too are expected to decrease by 2.22 percent. Once the new values of ρ are determined for all bonds at this lower level, the corresponding values of the semiannually compounded discount rate ρ' can be derived using the relationship $\rho' = e^\rho - 1$. The corresponding end-of-the-month values of the annualized rates $2\rho'$ are shown in column 3 of Table 4.7.

Next we ought to determine the expected end-of-period stock prices, assuming that the value of the whole market portfolio rises by 1/12 of 35 percent, or in other words by 2.92 percent. To that end, we must first determine the monthly compounded risk-free rate of return r'_{12} that is equivalent to the annually compounded rate $2r'$, by means of the following formula:

$$r'_{12} = (1 + 2r')^{1/12} - 1, \tag{4.55}$$
$$= (1.0725)^{1/12} - 1,$$
$$= 0.585\%.$$

Table 4.7

#	ending t(sem)	ending 2ρ'(%)	ending S($)	ending b(%)	coupon payment	total ending value	origin. b(%)	annual period return	#
1	28.98	9.00	47.36	146.90	2.50	149.40	144.13	43.92	2
2	23.83	8.82	19.53	140.65	0.00	140.65	137.38	28.58	6
3	32.47	9.05	92.28	211.70	0.00	211.70	205.62	35.44	3
4	12.95	8.66	127.22	193.79	5.50	199.29	194.21	31.34	4
5	23.19	8.82	23.61	121.00	0.00	121.00	118.00	30.49	5
6	4.28	8.48	46.88	97.48	0.00	97.48	96.52	11.92	10
7	28.14	8.96	114.70	365.56	0.00	365.56	351.58	47.71	1
8	9.62	8.60	52.32	116.35	0.00	116.35	113.86	26.21	7
9	13.83	8.69	34.12	105.71	0.00	105.71	103.50	25.62	8
10	16.99	8.73	33.73	91.29	2.50	93.79	91.97	23.70	9

Based on the fundamental property of the capital asset pricing model that relates the expected return on any individual stock to that on the market as a whole, the expected monthly return on the stock must be equal to:

$$r_{12}' + \beta[(0.35/12) - r_{12}'] = .00585 + .0233\beta \tag{4.56}$$

The numerical value of this monthly rate of change can easily be determined for any given stock by simply plugging the β-value of that stock into the right side of Equation 4.56. For example, since the β-value for the first bond considered in our numerical example is equal to 1.50, the monthly rate of change in the value of one share of its underlying stock equals .00585

+ (.0233) (1.50) = 4.0825 percent. As the current stock price is assumed to be \$45.5, the projected end-of-period stock price amounts to (45.5) (1.040825) = \$47.36. This figure shows up in the first row of column 4 in Table 4.7. The projected stock prices can be calculated in the same way for all other bonds.

It may seem at first sight that we used different risk-free rates of interest in Equations 4.53 and 4.56, even though both express the same fundamental relationship of the capital asset pricing model: the continuously compounded risk-free rate $2r$ shows up in Equation 4.53, while the monthly compounded risk-free rate r'_{12} is used in Equation 4.56. In fact there is no contradiction at all, as Equation 4.53 expresses the *instantaneous* rate of change in the stock price, while Equation 4.56 expresses the rate of change *over the period of one month*. Equation 4.56 should therefore tend to Equation 4.53 whenever the duration of the period of time under consideration tends to zero. This in fact turns out to be true, as it can be shown that the annualized periodically compounded rate converges to the continuously compounded rate $2r$ when smaller and smaller periods of time are considered.

Column 2 shows the remaining lives of the bonds in semesters after one month, or 1/6 of a semester, has passed. The projected end-of-month bond values, exclusive of any coupon payments made in the given month, are shown in column 5. Column 6 shows that only holders of bonds 1, 4, and 10 receive coupon payments during the month. These are added to the corresponding bond values of column 5 to obtain the total ending value of an investment made in those bonds in the beginning of the month. For the other bonds, the total ending value coincides with the bond value at the end of the month. All total ending values are shown in column 7. A comparison of these figures with the original bond values in the beginning of the month shown in column 8, leads to the expected annualized period returns in column 9. Finally, all bonds are ranked in the last column in order of decreasing expected period returns. A quick comparison with the ranks of Table 4.6, which were based on the order of magnitude of the expected annualized instantaneous returns, tells us that no bond has been ranked differently. This simply means that the time interval of one month proves to be small enough to preserve the bond ranks, despite the fact that the instantaneous rates of change of interest rates and stock prices were assumed to be markedly smaller than the corresponding period rates of change. This suggests that the instantaneous approach of the previous section can be considered a good approximation of the period approach of this section.

The analysis of both sections provides us with powerful methods of ranking different convertible bonds in a way that is consistent with the investor's expectations about the future course of interest rates and stock prices. The method can also easily be applied on a microcomputer, using either a specialized program or a suitable spreadsheet template. Assuming that all the primary convertible bond data have been provided to the microcomputer, such a program or template should enable the investor to rank all bonds in just a matter of seconds, and should provide him with all the bond characteristics discussed in this chapter. That way, ranking the bonds would hardly take more time than is necessary to update the primary data and to provide them to the computer. In fact, only five convertible bond features need to be updated on a regular basis. Two of them are straight bond features, namely the maturity and the applicable discount rate of the bond. The remaining three are related to the underlying stock: its price, its volatility, and its β-value. The volatility and the β-value are fairly stable, and therefore need not be updated as quickly as the stock price. To the degree that the volatility is derived from the convertible bond price quotation, this quotation rather than the volatility itself must regularly be updated. In addition to these five convertible bond features, only the risk-free rate of interest, the expectations with respect to its future course, and the expected return on the stock market as a whole need regular updating as well.

THE RISK FACTOR

So far, we have taken into account only expected rates of change in interest rates and stock prices, without considering any uncertainty the investor may have about these expectations. This uncertainty causes investments in convertible bonds to be risky and, in principle, risk should be a major concern of any investor.

A simple way of taking risk into account is to consider three different levels of change in the value of the stock market as a whole and in the risk-free rate of interest. The first of these levels reflects an optimistic view, the second one a pessimistic view, while the third corresponds to the most likely scenario. For each of these levels, corresponding rates of return on the convertible bonds can be figured out. This way, optimistic, pessimistic, and most likely returns are obtained for each of the bonds considered, which should give the investor some idea of the risk involved in selecting them. In general, bonds may get different ranks, depending on which scenario is considered. Under those circumstances, bonds must be assigned final ranks by considering all levels of bond returns simultaneously, and by making a judgment as to their relative merits.

In order to proceed in a more explicit and systematic way, one may first assign subjective probabilities of occurrence to the optimistic, pessimistic, and most likely scenarios, then multiply these probabilities by the bond returns that correspond to these scenarios, and finally add up these three products to obtain *weighted average* bond returns, with weights equal to the scenario probabilities. These weighted average bond returns can be interpreted as the return levels that are expected on a prior basis, before it is known which scenario will actually occur. Bonds can then be given ranks based on these weighted average returns, as well as on the possible deviations of the actual returns from these average returns.

The weighted average return of any bond in fact represents the *mean* of the probability distribution of the return of that bond. The possible outcomes of such a distribution coincide with the bond returns derived in each of the three scenarios. In more sophisticated approaches, many more possible scenarios would be considered, that is many more different rates of change in interest rates and many more different rates of change in the value of the stock market portfolio. Probabilities are to be assigned to each possible combination of these rates of change in interest rates and stock prices, reflecting the investor's degree of belief in their occurrence. As two different rates of change are involved, the corresponding probability distribution is called a *joint* distribution. From this joint distribution, one could then derive a probability distribution for the return of each of the bonds considered, that would generally have as many different outcomes as the underlying joint distribution. Finally, the distributions of all bond returns must be compared as to their relative merits.

Although the concept of probability distribution is a powerful tool in theoretical analyses of the bond selection problem, it is hard to use this concept in practical applications whenever many parameters of such a distribution need to be estimated. A more operational approach consists of considering only two characteristics of such a probability distribution, namely its *mean* and its *standard deviation*. The mean is then interpreted as the expected value, while the standard deviation represents the degree of dispersion of the probability distribution around the mean. The standard deviation, therefore, is usually considered an appropriate measure of the uncertainty or the risk involved. The square of the standard deviation is commonly known as the *variance*. To the degree that joint distributions are analyzed, additional characteristics must be considered, namely the *covariances,* which measure the degree of correlation between the stochastic variables.

One model in which this approach is taken is Markowitz's portfolio selection model. This model explains how an optimal portfolio of securities can be determined, assuming that the expected values, standard deviations, and the covariances of their returns are given. The toughest part of implementing the model in practical applications is the estimation of these characteristics of the joint distribution of the returns on the given securities. The portfolio approach does not aim in the first place at assigning ranks to the bonds, but at determining which fractions of the investor's capital should be invested in the different bonds considered. In other words, this approach not only tells the investor *which bonds* to invest his money in, but also tells him exactly *how much money* to invest in each bond. In principle, the portfolio model should not be applied to just convertible bonds, but to all securities that an investor is considering in his investment decisions. A convertible bond fund manager, however, would only apply it to convertible bonds, while ignoring all other securities. As a detailed description of the way in which Markowitz's model can be applied to convertible bond selection is beyond the scope of this text, we will confine ourselves to a brief outline of the general ideas without any numerical illustration, and without considering any other type of securities than convertible bonds.

Assume that a portfolio manager must decide how to allocate his investment capital to K different convertible bonds.

In other words, assume that he must determine what fractions of his capital to invest in these K different bonds. If a particular bond is not to be considered for investment, the fraction allocated to that bond is simply zero. If the fraction to be invested in the kth bond is denoted by x_k, and if R_{b_k} and R_p respectively represent the expected annualized instantaneous returns on the kth bond and on the portfolio, the following relationship can be established:

$$R_p = \sum_{k=1}^{K} x_k R_{b_k}, \tag{4.57}$$

where, in conformity with Equation 4.50, R_{b_k} is determined by:

$$R_{b_k} = e(b_k, s_k) R_{s_k} + e(b_k, r) R_r + [2(\rho_k i_k - ro_{2,k})/b_k]. \tag{4.58}$$

In this latter equation, R_{s_k} denotes the expected annualized instantaneous return on the stock underlying the kth bond, $e(b_k, s_k)$ and $e(b_k, r)$ denote the elasticities of the kth bond value with respect to changes in the value of its underlying stock and in the risk-free rate of interest, and b_k, ρ_k, i_k, and $o_{2,k}$ respectively denote the values b, ρ, i, and o_2 of the kth bond.

In view of Equation 4.53, R_{s_k} can be specified as follows:

$$R_{s_k} = 2r + \beta_k (R_m - 2r), \tag{4.59}$$

where β_k stands for the β-value of the kth bond, and R_m for the expected return on the stock market portfolio. By substituting the right side of Equation 4.59 for R_{s_k} in Equation 4.58, we obtain the following alternative expression for the expected return on the bond:

$$R_{b_k} = e(b_k, s_k)\beta_k R_m + e(b_k, r)R_r + 2re(b_k, s_k)(1 - \beta_k)$$
$$+ [2(\rho_k i_k - ro_{2,k})/b_k]. \tag{4.60}$$

Finally, the standard deviation σ_p of the portfolio return can be shown to be equal to:

$$\sigma_p = \left[\sum_{k=1}^{K} \sum_{l=1}^{K} x_k x_l \sigma_{kl}^b \right]^{1/2}, \qquad (4.61)$$

where σ_{kl}^b represents the covariance of the instantaneous returns on bonds k and l , which in turn is derived from the following equation:

$$\sigma_{kl}^b = e(b_k, s_k)\, e(b_l, s_l)\, \sigma_{kl}^s + e(b_k, r)\, e(b_l, r)\, \sigma_r^2$$
$$+ \; e(b_k, s_k)\, e(b_l, r)\, \sigma_{kr} + e(b_l, s_l)\, e(b_k, r)\, \sigma_{lr}. \qquad (4.62)$$

The factor σ_r represents in this expression the standard deviation of the rate of change in r, σ_{kl}^s stands for the covariance of the instantaneous returns on stocks k and l, σ_{kr} and σ_{lr} denote the covariances of the rate of interest r and the returns on stocks k and l, respectively, while $e(b_l, s_l)$ and $e(b_l, r)$ are the stock price and interest elasticities of the value of bond l.

In view of the large number of variances and covariances to be estimated in Equations 4.61 and 4.62, one may prefer to derive approximate results from a smaller number of parameters within the framework of an *index model*, referred to in the introduction to this chapter. Equation 4.60 suggests that we should use two indices in this approach, namely the return R_m on the market portfolio and the rate of change R_r in the risk-free rate of interest r. If we represent the covariance of the deviations of the actual rates of return on stocks k and l from their theoretical values on the characteristic line by σ_{kl}^ϵ , the covariance of the return on the market portfolio and the rate of change in r by σ_{mr}, the standard deviation of the market return by σ_m , and the standard deviation of the rate of change in r by σ_r , we can derive the following approximate value of σ_{kl}^b within the index model based on these two indices[5]:

$$\sigma_{kl}^b = e(b_k, s_k)\, e(b_l, s_l)\, \beta_k \beta_l \sigma_m^2 + e(b_k, r)\, e(b_l, r)\, \sigma_r^2$$
$$+ [e(b_k, s_k)\, e(b_l, r)\, \beta_k + e(b_l, s_l)\, e(b_k, r)\, \beta_l]\, \sigma_{mr}$$
$$+ e(b_k, s_k)\, e(b_l, s_l)\, \sigma_{kl}^\epsilon, \tag{4.63}$$

where it is assumed that $\sigma_{kl}^\epsilon = 0$ whenever k and l do not refer to the same stock. Comparing Equation 4.63 with Equation 4.62 leads to the conclusion that the number of parameters to be estimated has drastically been reduced. The only parameters to be estimated are the expected market return R_m, the β factors, the expected rate of change R_r of the risk-free interest rate, the standard deviations σ_m, σ_r, the covariance σ_{mr}, and the residual terms σ_{kl}^ϵ *for* $k = l$. Once these parameters are estimated, the corresponding expected value and standard deviation of the portfolio return can be derived for any given set of distribution fractions x_k from Equations 4.57, 4.60, 4.61, and 4.63. Different sets of fractions x_k lead to different combinations of expected portfolio return and associated portfolio risk, as measured by the standard deviation of that return. All combinations need to be compared and the best combination must be selected. That best combination will always be located on the *efficient frontier,* which represents the set of portfolios with minimum risk, given their level of expected return, and with maximum expected return, given their level of risk. Portfolios on this efficient frontier with higher expected returns are also more risky. The frontier itself can be determined by means of a suitable computer program that is based on the optimization techniques described in Markowitz's model. If a risk-free security is considered as part of the portfolio, the efficient frontier contains all combinations of the risk-free security and an optimal portfolio of convertible bonds. Once the efficient frontier is determined, the ultimate selection of a portfolio on that efficient frontier can be made either in an intuitive way, or by determining the investor's utility function over the set of all possible combinations of expected returns and standard deviations, and then maximizing the utility function over the efficient frontier. Although the concept of utility function is very useful in theoretical analyses, it is hard to determine that function in practice. The best approach in practical applications therefore consists in just determining the efficient frontier, and to make the final selection on the basis of sound judgment and one's own attitude toward risk.

NOTES

1. The phrase "return on the straight bond investment" is here used to indicate the return that would be earned on an investment in a straight bond with characteristics equal to the corresponding straight bond characteristics of the convertible bond.

2. If no dividend payments occur at the very moment at which instantaneous changes or returns are considered, they can safely be ignored in the definition of the rate of return on the stock, which therefore coincides with the rate of change of its price. Similarly, when period returns are considered, no distinction need be made between the rate of return on the stock and the rate of change of its price, as long as no dividend payments occur in the period under consideration. However, even when dividend payments do not occur at the moment or during the period considered, they would still affect the option values at those times and therefore also the corresponding return on the conversion option and on the bond. For the sake of simplicity, we will nevertheless ignore the impact of dividend payments on option and bond returns in this chapter.

3. β can more formally be defined as the ratio of the covariance of the individual stock and market portfolio returns over the variance of the market portfolio return.

4. Strictly speaking, this fundamental relationship only applies to stock markets in equilibrium. Should the stock market not be in equilibrium, then an additional term must be added to the right side of the relationship, that is usually referred to as the "alpha" of the

stock, which is positive (negative) when the stock is underpriced (overpriced). Equation 4.53 can therefore be considered an equilibrium condition, that must be satisfied by all stocks whenever the market is in equilibrium. It is usually referred to as the *security market line*.

5. Equation 4.63 is only correct within the assumptions of the index model, according to which a zero value is taken by the covariances of the rate of change of the risk-free rate of interest, and of the return on the market portfolio, with the deviation of any individual stock return from its theoretical value. The simplification inherent in the index model is directly related to this assumption. To the degree that it is incorrect, Equation 4.63 provides only approximate values for σ^b_{kl}.

5

Convertible Euro-Bonds

INTRODUCTION

Euro-bonds could be defined as *bonds that are underwritten by an international syndicate or management group and that are issued principally in countries other than the country of the issuer.* Typically, they are issued in several countries at a time, and the currency in which they are denominated may or may not be the currency of the country of the issuer. Whenever such a Euro-bond is convertible into shares of common stock of the issuing company, it is referred to as a *convertible Euro-bond.* Such a convertible Euro-bond may or may not be denominated in the same currency as its underlying common stock. If it is not, a clear distinction must be made between the two currencies involved. The currency in which the bond is denominated will in this chapter be referred to as the *bond currency* (C_b), while the currency in which the underlying stock is denominated will be called the *stock currency* (C_s). If both currencies differ, a currency clause will always stipulate a *nominal exchange rate* for the two currencies involved, that is to be applied at the time of conversion.

This nominal exchange rate generally differs from the current *market* exchange rate, as the former is fixed for the life of the conversion option, while the latter varies on a continuing basis whenever the foreign exchange markets are in operation. This disparity between nominal and market exchange rates is a risk factor of investments in convertible Euro-bonds that does not affect investments in domestic bonds.

Obviously, the disparity between nominal and market exchange rates does not exist whenever bond and stock currencies coincide. This is the case, for example, when a British firm issues sterling-denominated convertible bonds in continental Europe. In such a case both nominal and market exchange rates are identically equal to 1. This kind of convertible bonds therefore only represents a special category of Euro-bonds, which can be treated in exactly the same way as Euro-bonds with different bond and stock currencies.

To the degree that we want to compare convertible Euro-bonds that are denominated in different currencies, we need to use a single *reference currency*, in terms of which the values of bonds with different currency denominations can be expressed. When it comes to valuing and selecting convertible Euro-bonds, the obvious choice of such a reference currency is the currency of the investor's country. For a U.S. investor, therefore, the obvious choice is the U.S. dollar. As, in addition, the U.S. dollar is the most widely used international currency, we will use it as the reference currency throughout this chapter.

In view of the role played by the reference currency, three different currencies have to be considered when convertible Euro-bonds are valued and selected, namely the bond currency, the stock currency, and the reference currency. Furthermore, the return realized on an investment in a convertible Euro-bond after a certain holding period generally depends on two different exchange rates, namely the exchange rate between the bond and stock currencies on one hand, and the exchange rate between the bond currency and the reference currency on the other. For example, if a U.S. investor invests money in bonds that are denominated in German marks and are convertible into yen-denominated shares of common stock of a Japanese company, his holding period return will depend on the period fluctuation of the exchange rate between Japanese yen and German marks, as well as on the period fluctuation of the exchange rate between German marks and U.S. dollars.

We will show in this chapter that the analysis of the preceding chapters can easily be extended to include convertible Euro-bonds. In fact, we only need to integrate this new dimension of currency exchange rate fluctuations and the previous dimensions of interest rate and stock price fluctuations. Since the extended international model includes the previous model for the convertible bonds of the domestic type as a special case, it can be used to value and rank all bonds in any mixed set of international and domestic convertible bonds. In order to do so, it suffices to set nominal and market exchange rates between bond and stock currencies on one hand, and the market exchange rate between bond and reference currencies on the other hand, equal to 1 for the domestic bonds.

Like the domestic model, the international model can also be applied to mixed sets of convertible and straight bonds, as straight bonds can be considered a special case of a convertible bond. All it takes to include straight bonds in the analysis is to assume an infinitely large conversion price for these straight bonds (or a zero number of shares to be obtained in exchange for them), while margin payments can conveniently be set equal to zero. As a practical matter, such an infinitely large conversion price must be approximated on the computer by a very large number (e.g., the largest power of 10 that both hardware and software can handle). In the extended model of this chapter, one could also set the nominal exchange rate equal to zero (or an extremely small number of) units of the stock currency for one unit of the bond currency. Either of these parameter values results in a zero option value for the straight bonds. This way, the value of any straight bond always coincides with the investment value that can be derived within the convertible bond valuation model, when that straight bond is treated as a special kind of convertible bond. In order to make this investment value correspond to the observed market value of such a straight bond, it suffices to set its discount rate ρ equal to its yield to maturity at the given straight bond price.

Summing up, *the model of this chapter can be used to manage any mixed portfolio of domestic, international, straight, and convertible bonds,* and enables the portfolio manager to rank all of them in order of magnitude of their expected returns. This international model could also be extended to include risk considerations on the basis of Markowitz's portfolio optimization techniques, in the same way in which the domestic model was extended at the end of Chapter 4.

THE EURO-BOND MODEL

As in the previous chapter, we will again use a numerical example to clarify the valuation and selection techniques of this chapter and, for convenience, we will again assume that only 10 different bonds need to be ranked. It is obvious that many more bonds may be considered in practical applications, but with a suitable computer program, it should not take much more time to rank large numbers of them, except for the fact that more data would have to be provided to the computer. Many parameters in the following illustration are assumed to take the same values as in the previous illustration, namely the redemption values, the maturities, the side payments, and the β-values. However, the coupon rates, the conversion prices, the current stock prices, and the bond price quotations are assumed to take different values. For convenience, we still assume that all bonds pay interest semiannually. Although many convertible Euro-bonds have annual coupons, this condition does not really restrict the applicability of the model to practical portfolio management, as it could easily be dropped as a nonessential feature of our numerical illustration.

We also need to point out that some parameters of the previous model no longer take the same value for all bonds considered. Thus the risk-free rate of interest will take different values for bonds denominated in different currencies. Basically, we no longer deal with a single risk-free rate of interest, but with as many rates as there are bond currencies. In addition, these interest rates can no longer be expected to change in the same direction or at the same rate, as the direction and the rate of change of interest rates in any given country will heavily depend on the particular political, economic, monetary, and financial position of that country. Furthermore, as the underlying stock of different Euro-bonds may be traded on different stock markets, we no longer can confine ourselves to a single domestic stock market. As these stock markets may move in different degrees, or even in different directions, we also have to consider different rates of return on the corresponding stock market portfolios.

Obviously, we also must introduce new parameters into the model that relate different currencies to each other. First, we must consider the exchange rate γ that represents the number of U.S. dollars that are currently being exchanged in the currency markets for one unit of the bond currency. This exchange rate will be referred to as the *bond exchange rate.*

Second, we also need to consider the exchange rate δ that represents the number of bond currency units that are currently being exchanged in the currency markets for one unit of the stock currency. This rate will henceforth be called the *conversion exchange rate.* The nominal value of this conversion exchange rate, referred to in the very beginning of this chapter, will be denoted by δ_n. Finally, a *stock exchange rate* ϵ is introduced that represents the number of U.S. dollars that can be obtained in the marketplace in exchange for one stock currency unit.

Note that these three different exchange rates are not independent of each other. In fact, they relate to each other according to the following formula:

$$\gamma\delta = \epsilon. \qquad (5.1)$$

In principle, therefore, we only need to consider two of these three exchange rates. Most of the time, we will treat γ and ϵ as independent exchange rates and $\delta = \epsilon/\gamma$ as a derived rate.

In addition to the exchange rates themselves, we also need to take into account the rates of change of these exchange rates. The instantaneous annualized rates of change of γ, δ, and ϵ will be denoted by R_γ, R_δ, and R_ϵ, respectively. In addition to an interest effect, a stock price effect, and a time effect on the bond return, we will also have to consider a *currency effect,* which represents the impact on the bond return of any changes in the currency exchange rates. This currency effect will obviously depend on the values of R_γ, R_δ, and R_ϵ.

The 10 columns of Table 5.2 contain the following sequence of data for each bond: the bond number, the annualized coupon rate $2c$, the redemption value v, the number of semesters to maturity t, the annualized discount rate $2\rho'$, the annually compounded risk-free rate of return $2r'$, the bond currency C_b, the number of bond currency units per

U.S. dollar $1/\gamma$, the stock currency C_s, and the number of stock currency units per U.S. dollar $1/\epsilon$. The only reason for considering $1/\gamma$ and $1/\epsilon$ instead of γ and ϵ is that exchange rates of foreign currencies are more customarily quoted as a number of foreign currency units per U.S. dollar than as a number of U.S. dollars per foreign currency unit. The different currencies used in our numerical illustration, their symbols, and their hypothetical current exchange rates against the U.S. dollar are shown in Table 5.1.

Table 5.1

Currency	symbol	$1/\gamma$ or $1/\delta$
U.S. dollar	$	1
Japanese yen	Y	171.36
German marks	DM	2.378
Pound sterling	P.st.	0.832
French francs	FF	7.049
Swiss francs	FS	1.896
Dutch guilders	Fl	2.517

These exchange rates represent the value of either $1/\gamma$ or $1/\epsilon$, depending on whether they correspond to bond currencies or to stock currencies. One currency in our numerical illustration shows up as a bond currency only, namely the pound sterling, while the yen and the Swiss franc only show up as stock currencies (Table 5.2). All other currencies considered serve as both bond and stock currencies.

All the figures in Table 5.2 represent raw data that must be provided to the computer, as do all figures of Table 5.3, except the δ-values that are derived from the corresponding γ-

Table 5.2

#	2c(%)	v(%)	t(sem)	2ρ̂(%)	2r'(%)	C_b	1/γ	C_s	1/ε
1	5	100	29.15	8.60	5.75	DM	2.378	Y	171.36
2	4³/⁸	102	24.00	10.53	8.25	$	1.000	$	1.000
3	6⁵/⁸	100	32.64	8.71	5.75	DM	2.378	Y	171.36
4	4¹/⁴	101	13.12	8.23	5.75	DM	2.378	$	1.000
5	6¹/⁴	100	23.36	12.17	9.50	FF	7.049	FF	7.049
6	3³/⁴	103	4.45	10.18	8.25	$	1.000	Y	171.36
7	10³/⁸	100	28.31	10.67	8.25	$	1.000	FS	1.896
8	6¹/²	100	9.79	12.64	10.25	P.st.	0.832	FF	7.049
9	3¹/²	99.5	14.00	8.46	6.00	Fl	2.517	Fl	2.517
10	5	100	17.16	12.81	10.25	P.st.	0.832	DM	2.378

and ϵ-values according to Equation 5.1. The columns in this third table respectively contain the bond numbers, the dimensions C_b/C_s of the conversion exchange rates, their numerical values δ, the nominal exchange rates δ_n, the conversion prices p_c, the margin payments m, the current stock prices S, and the current bond price quotations.

The figures in Table 5.4 are derived from all these data in Tables 5.2 and 5.3. To start with, the conversion values in the second column are determined as a fraction of the nominal bond value by the following approximate formula:

$$b_c = (S/p_c)(\delta/\delta_n) - m, \qquad (5.2)$$

where m represents the margin payments as a fraction of the

Table 5.3

#	C_b/C_s	δ	δ_n	P_c	m(%)	S	bond price(%)
1	DM/Y	0.014	0.011	8200 Y	0	9100 Y	$171^{3/4}$
2	$/$	1.000	1.000	28.50 $	0	12 $	$78^{1/2}$
3	DM/Y	0.014	0.011	11800 Y	18	17875 Y	$246^{1/4}$
4	DM/$	2.378	2.858	95 $	0	123 $	151
5	FF/FF	1.000	1.000	337.75 FF	0	108.5 FF	$87^{1/4}$
6	$/Y	0.006	0.004	15600 Y	$14^{3/4}$	9225 Y	$123^{1/2}$
7	$/FS	0.527	0.413	91.875 FS	0	167.25 FS	$342^{1/4}$
8	P.St./FF	0.118	0.086	385 FF	0	357 FF	$148^{1/2}$
9	Fl/Fl	1.000	1.000	178.25 Fl	10	75.9 Fl	$91^{3/4}$
10	P.St./DM	0.350	0.264	300 DM	0	82.5 DM	$91^{1/4}$

nominal bond value. The next column contains the square roots σ of the stock volatilities implied by the bond price quotations in the last column of Table 5.3. These implied volatilities can be derived from the given bond price quotations by trial and error or suitable computer programs, as explained in Chapter 4.[1] Columns 4, 5, and 6 show the investment values, the option values, and the bond values, respectively, while the interest and stock price elasticities of the bond values are shown in columns 7 and 8. There is no need to adjust any of the formulas underlying the figures in columns 3 through 8, as the conversion values of the bonds in column 2 are expressed as a fraction of the corresponding

Table 5.4

#	b_c(%)	σ	i(%)	o(%)	b(%)	e_r^b	e_s^b
1	140.00	.281838	72.53	101.35	173.87	-0.18	0.76
2	42.11	.336452	59.19	19.31	78.50	-0.52	0.40
3	173.11	.491866	83.19	164.25	247.44	-0.20	0.74
4	107.73	.604714	82.59	70.28	152.87	-0.19	0.60
5	32.12	.668508	65.57	23.68	89.25	-0.58	0.31
6	71.52	.757862	90.90	33.63	124.53	-0.12	0.47
7	244.99	1.43723	101.42	244.41	345.83	-0.22	0.71
8	127.26	.326765	78.75	70.43	149.18	-0.12	0.78
9	32.58	.562242	73.92	17.83	91.75	-0.36	0.30
10	36.45	1.02916	62.13	31.22	93.35	-0.50	0.36

nominal bond values in conformity with the procedure followed for domestic bonds.

Next, consider the figures in columns 3, 4, 5, 6, and 8 in Table 5.5. They represent instantaneous annualized rates of change of the risk-free rate of interest r,[2] the bond exchange rate γ, the stock exchange rate ϵ, the value of the market portfolio, and the individual stock price S,[3] respectively. The changes in r, γ, ϵ, and in the value of the market portfolio are considered to be autonomous. The rate R_r is in fact derived from the number of basis points $\Delta(2r')$ by which the annually compounded interest rate $2r'$ is changing, according to the following formula:

Table 5.5

#	$\Delta(2r')$	R_r (%)	R_γ (%)	R_ϵ (%)	R_m (%)	β	R_s (%)
1	75	12.69	20	30	25	1.50	34.70
2	150	17.48	0	0	-15	0.95	-13.85
3	75	12.69	20	30	25	1.14	27.72
4	75	12.69	20	0	-15	1.22	-19.53
5	200	20.13	10	10	-21	1.13	-24.91
6	150	17.48	0	30	25	0.45	15.61
7	150	17.48	0	22	13	1.78	16.96
8	100	9.30	-15	10	-21	0.86	-16.96
9	75	12.14	18	18	19	1.20	21.63
10	100	9.30	-15	20	11	0.70	10.63

$$R_r = \frac{\Delta(2r')/10,000}{(1 + 2r')\ln(1 + 2r')} . \tag{5.3}$$

The hypothetical values of $\Delta(2r')$ are shown in the second column of Table 5.5, and differ from one currency to another. On the other hand, the returns R_s in column 8 on the individual underlying stocks are derived from the hypothetical expected return R_m on the stock market portfolio to which they belong, and from their corresponding β-value in column 7, in conformity with the following fundamental relationship of the capital asset pricing model:

$$R_s = 2r + \beta(R_m - 2r), \tag{5.4}$$

where β measures the sensitivity of any underlying stock to movements in the stock market portfolio *of the country of the issuer of that stock*. In other words, the β-value of any given stock has to be determined relative to the stock market where it is traded. If the same stock is traded on different stock markets, the relevant market to be considered is the one in the country of the issuer of the underlying stock, as this is normally the market that dictates the price of that stock to other markets.

It should also be pointed out that we can no longer consider uniform rates of change R_r and R_m, as R_r will normally differ from one currency to another and R_m will normally differ from one stock market to another. Both rates of change must therefore be defined on a country-by-country basis, in the same way as the rates of change in γ and ϵ. More specifically, the rates of change for the different countries that underly the figures in columns 2 through 6 in Table 5.5, are shown in Table 5.6.

The figures in columns 2, 3, and 4 of Table 5.6 show up in the same columns of Table 5.5 for the different *bond* currencies involved, while the figures in columns 4 and 5 of Table 5.6 equal the corresponding figures in columns 5 and 6 of Table 5.5 for the different *stock* currencies involved.

Finally, the impact of all these changes on the bond return is shown in Table 5.7. In addition to the stock price effect, the interest effect, and the time effect that we considered in the previous chapter, we must now consider a *currency effect* as well. This currency effect represents the cumulative impact on the bond return of changes in both the bond exchange rate and the conversion exchange rate. It can be shown to equal the sum

$$R_\gamma + e_s^b R_\delta, \tag{5.5}$$

which must be added to all other effects to obtain the total

Table 5.6

Country	$\Delta(2r')$	R_r	R_γ or R_ϵ	R_m
U.S.A.	150 points	17.48%	0%	-15%
Japan	n.a.	n.a.	30%	25%
Germany	75 points	12.69%	20%	11%
Great Britain	100 points	9.30%	-15%	n.a.
France	200 points	20.13%	10%	-21%
Switzerland	n.a.	n.a.	22%	13%
The Netherlands	75 points	12.14%	18%	19%

bond return. Since e_s^b normally is smaller than 1, this expression clearly shows that *the impact on the bond return of a given percentage rate of change in the bond exchange rate is stronger than the impact of the same percentage rate of change in the conversion exchange rate.* The value of R_δ can be derived from the given values of R_γ and R_ϵ in the following way:

$$R_\delta = R_\epsilon - R_\gamma. \qquad (5.6)$$

By substituting the right side of this equation for R_δ in Equation 5.5 and rearranging terms, we can also express the currency effect as the following function of R_γ and R_ϵ:

$$(1 - e_s^b) R_\gamma + e_s^b R_\epsilon. \qquad (5.7)$$

Since e_s^b normally is a number between 0 and 1, this expression clearly shows that *the currency effect is a weighted average of the rates of change in the bond and stock exchange rates.*

Table 5.7

#	currency effect	stock price effect	interest effect	time effect	R_i (%)	R_o (%)	R_b (%)	#
1	27.62	26.44	-2.31	2.51	-1.56	59.88	54.26	1
2	0.00	-5.49	-9.06	6.55	-5.07	-17.00	-8.00	10
3	27.38	20.44	-2.56	2.45	-1.64	42.57	47.71	2
4	7.97	-11.75	-2.41	3.56	2.38	-52.02	-2.63	8
5	10.00	-7.77	-11.75	8.26	-5.52	-27.13	-1.26	7
6	13.97	7.27	-2.09	5.70	6.23	75.15	24.84	5
7	15.57	12.00	-3.29	3.04	-3.02	39.02	26.69	3
8	4.46	-12.99	-1.13	3.48	7.54	10.24	-6.18	9
9	18.00	6.52	-4.43	6.05	2.13	33.05	26.14	4
10	-2.34	3.84	-4.64	8.00	5.12	49.19	4.86	6

The currency effect for the different bonds is shown in column 2 of Table 5.7, while the figures in columns 3, 4, and 5 represent the stock price effects, the interest effects, and the time effects, respectively. These latter effects are determined in exactly the same way as in the previous chapter. Columns 6 and 7 contain the corresponding rates of change in the investment values and in the option values as a fraction of the nominal values. While the investment values are not affected by changes in the exchange rates, the option values do change in response to a change in the conversion exchange rate δ. For any given rate of change R_δ, the option value o will change at a rate equal to $e_s^o R_\delta$. This currency factor has been taken into account in determining the figures in column 7.

By adding all of the four different effects, we obtain the expected bond return:

$$R_b = (1 - e_s^b) R_\gamma + e_s^b R_\epsilon + e_s^b R_s + e_r^b R_r + [2(\rho i - o_2 r)/b], \tag{5.8}$$

$$= [(i - o_2)R_\gamma + o_1 R_\epsilon + o_1 R_s - (i\rho d - o_2 rt)R_r + 2(\rho i - o_2 r)]/b. \tag{5.9}$$

Alternatively, it can also be derived from R_i, R_o, and R_γ, according to the following formula:

$$R_b = R_\gamma + (i/b)R_i + (o/b)R_o, \tag{5.10}$$

where

$$R_i = (2 - dR_r)\,\rho \tag{5.11}$$

and

$$R_o = e_s^o R_\delta + e_s^o R_s + e_r^o R_r - (o_2/o)(2r), \tag{5.12}$$

$$= [o_1 R_\delta + o_1 R_s - (2 - tR_r)\,o_2 r]/o. \tag{5.13}$$

The values for R_b are shown in column 8, while column 9 shows the different ranks of the bonds based on the order of magnitude of these expected bond returns. Bond 1 turns out to have the best rank, with an expected annualized return of 54.26 percent, while bond 2 is expected to perform worst, with a negative expected return of -8 percent per year.

As indicated in Chapter 4, we could again consider period returns and period rates of change instead of instantaneous returns and instantaneous rates of change. We could again take risk into account by considering three different scenarios: an optimistic one, a pessimistic one, and a most likely one. And, in principle, we could also apply Markowitz's portfolio model again to take fully into account the risk-reducing effect of diversification. This approach, however, is more complicated when applied to convertible Euro-bonds than when applied to domestic convertible bonds, as we must now consider the standard deviations and the pairwise covariances of (1) the rates of change of all relevant bond and stock exchange rates, (2) the rates of change of all relevant risk-free rates of interest, and (3) of the expected returns on all relevant stocks. As in Chapter 4, the analysis could dramatically be simplified within the context of a *multi-index model*. However, whereas only two indices were required in Chapter 4, we might need many more in an international context to account for all the different currencies and stock exchange markets under consideration. Therefore, even within this simplified approach, the number of parameters to be estimated may become very large if many different countries are involved, and the data required for determining all these estimates may not readily be available. Practical problems of this nature make it more difficult to apply the portfolio approach to international bonds than to domestic bonds, even though this approach is perfectly suitable for such applications on purely theoretical grounds.

NOTES

1. Note, however, that the volatilities σ^2 in Chapters 4 and 5 have a somewhat different meaning. In Chapter 4, the volatility was interpreted as the expected variability of stock price (expressed in stock currency). In the present chapter, on the other hand, it must be interpreted as the expected variability of the value of the stock *in terms of the bond currency*. It is obvious that this latter variability no longer exclusively depends on stock price movements, but also on fluctuations in the exchange rate δ between stock and bond currencies.

2. In conformity with Chapter 4, we again assume that the risk-free rates of interest r, as well as the discount rates ρ for any given

risk-class, can take different values at different points in time. For the sake of simplicity, however, they are also assumed again to have a constant term structure at one and the same point in time.

3. As in the previous chapter, we again simplifty the analysis by ignoring any dividend payments during the life of the conversion option. In view thereof, the rate of change of the value of any particular stock, or of any stock market portfolio, is identical to the rate of return on that stock or on that stock market portfolio, respectively.

6

Concluding Comments

In the previous chapters, we laid the analytic foundation of convertible bond management on the basis of modern straight bond and stock option theories. The numerical illustrations showed that the techniques described in these chapters do work. The present model, like any other, admittedly has its limitations. It could, for example, be extended to include dividend payments on the underlying stock, income and capital gain taxes, callability and other special features, transaction costs, more detailed aspects of the role of risk, and certain generalizations of the option and straight bond valuation models underlying the present analysis (such as those resulting from relaxing the assumptions of a constant stock volatility, a constant risk-free rate of interest, and a constant bond discount rate).

The analysis of these and other extensions is, however, beyond the scope of the present text. Some of the above complications were discussed in Chapters 3 and 4, but were not actually taken into account in the development of the model. Some extensions could be realized in a relatively easy way, others only with great difficulty. We noted, for example, that no extended Black-Scholes formula is currently available for callable coupon-bearing convertible bonds with finite maturity. In addition, some of the extensions, like a full-scaled risk-expected return model, are not very difficult to conceive at the theoretical level, but are relatively hard to implement in practice.

Despite these limitations, we believe that the present analysis is both theoretically well founded and practically oriented, and that it provides convertible bond managers with specific guidelines based on state-of-the-art techniques, that are far superior to the simple techniques commonly used in current investment practice. These guidelines indicate how convertible bonds can be selected on the basis of their expected return, and methods of extending the model to include risk considerations were outlined at the end of Chapter 4. As noted before, it should also be emphasized that the present analysis not only applies to domestic convertible bond management, but also to the management of any portfolio of straight, convertible, domestic, and international bonds. Finally, it is worthwhile mentioning that at least one special feature was explicitly taken into account—namely, the possible requirement that the bondholder must make some side payments at conversion—while we also provided formulas for valuing bonds that outlive their conversion option.

We hope that this work may stimulate others to remove some of the above limitations within the approach of the present analysis, and that it may contribute to a better understanding of convertible bonds in general. A better understanding, we believe, would lead to a more widespread use of these hybrids, both by investors as a suitable vehicle for meeting specific investment objectives and by corporations as a suitable instrument for satisfying specific financing needs.

Glossary

Accrued interest: prorated coupon interest earned on a bond since the last coupon date.

American option: a call or put option that can be execised on or before its expiration date.

Beta value: the covariance between the return on any individual security and the return on the market portfolio, as a fraction of the variance of the return on the market portfolio.

Black-Scholes valuation model: a well-known valuation model for regular stock options that was developed by Fischer Black and Myron Scholes in the early 1970s. The model can also be applied to the conversion option of a convertible bond.

Bond currency (convertible Euro-bonds): the currency in which a convertible Euro-bond is denominated.

Bond exchange rate (convertible Euro-bonds): the number of units of a reference currency that are currently exchanged in the currency markets for one unit of the bond currency.

Bond value: the total value of a convertible bond.

Callability: a feature of most convertible bonds, in which the issuer of the bonds has the option to redeem the bonds on certain terms during a certain period of time.

Call option: a right to buy a specific asset (usually a stock) at a specific fixed price. An American call option can be exercised on or before a specified expiration date, while a European call option can only be exercised at expiration. A special case of such a call option is the conversion option of a convertible bond, which entitles the bondholder to acquire a specified stock in exchange for that bond rather than for money, at a price that is specified in terms of nominal bond value instead of currency units.

Call price: the price at which a callable convertible bond can be redeemed at the option of the issuer of the bond.

Capital asset pricing model: a well-known pricing model for capital assets that was developed by John Lintner and William Sharpe in the 1960s.

Characteristic line: a straight line that represents a linear relationship between the expected return on any individual security and the expected return on the market portfolio.

Conversion exchange rate (convertible Euro-bonds): the number of bond currency units that are currently exchanged in the currency markets for one unit of the stock currency.

Conversion line: a straight line that represents a linear relationship between the conversion value of a convertible bond and the share price of its underlying stock.

Conversion option: a feature of a convertible bond that entitles its holder to exchange the bond for a specific number of shares of a specified common stock during a certain period of time. Sometimes the holder of the bond is required to pay a certain amount of money to the issuer when this option is exercised.

Conversion period: the period of time during which a conversion option can be exercised.

Conversion premium: the relative amount by which the total (market) value of a convertible bond exceeds its conversion value, i.e., the difference between the bond's total (market) value and its conversion value, as a fraction of the latter.

Conversion price: the total nominal value of a convertible bond to be exchanged for one share of underlying common stock at conversion.

Conversion ratio: the unrounded number of shares of common stock that can be obtained per unit ($1,000) of nominal bond value at conversion.

Conversion value: the current market value of all shares of common stock that can be obtained in exchange for a convertible bond through immediate conversion, minus the amount of any accompanying side payments by the bondholder.

Currency effect (convertible Euro-bonds): the component of any investment return related to exchange rate changes. For example, the total return on a convertible Euro-bond has such a component.

Duration: a weighted average maturity of the whole stream of cash payments to which the holder of a convertible bond is entitled during its remaining life, the weights being the present values of these cash payments as a fraction of the bond's investment value.

Efficient frontier: the collection of portfolios of any given securities, such that no other portfolio with an least the same expected return has a smaller risk, and such that no other portfolio with at most the same risk has a higher expected return.

European option: a call or put option that can only be exercised at expiration.

Excess value: the difference between the total value and the floor value of a regular stock option or a conversion option.

Exercise price: the fixed price at which an option can be exercised.

Floor value: a minimum value of a regular stock option or a conversion option before its expiration date; a minimum value for a convertible bond before the expiration date of its conversion option.

Hedge ratio: the change in the value of a call option on a stock, or of a bond that is convertible into that stock, as a fraction of any underlying change in the stock's share price.

Index model: a simplified version of Markowitz' portfolio selection model that relates the return of all individual securities to one or more common factors. Single-index models are based on only one factor, while multi-index models specify at least two factors.

Interest effect: the component of any investment return that is related to interest rate changes. For example, the total return on a convertible bond, the return on its straight bond investment, and the return on its conversion option have such a component.

Interest elasticity: the relative change in the investment value, option value, or total value of a convertible bond, as a fraction of any underlying relative change in interest rates.

Intrinsic value: the value that a nonexpiring regular stock option or conversion option would have if it were expiring; the value that a convertible bond would have if its conversion option were expiring.

Investment value: the value of the straight bond characteristics of a convertible bond, that is, the value that such a bond would have without its conversion feature.

Margin payments: the amount of money that an investor may be required to pay when converting a bond into its underlying stock.

Market portfolio: the portfolio of all outstanding shares of a given set of securities (e.g., all stocks traded on the New York Stock Exchange), or a scaled-down version of it.

Markowitz' portfolio selection model: a model for determining optimal security portfolios that was developed by Harry Markowitz in the 1950s.

Nominal bond value: the face value of a bond.

Nominal exchange rate (convertible Euro-bonds): the fixed exchange rate between bond and stock currencies stipulated on a convertible Euro-bond.

Non-diversifiable risk: the component of the total risk of a security portfolio that cannot be diversified away, that is, the component of the total portfolio risk that is exclusively related to movements in the security market as a whole.

Option value: the value of the conversion option of a convertible bond.

Par value: the face value of a bond.

Parity value: the value that a nonexpiring option would have if it were expiring.

Premium over investment value: the relative amount by which the total (market) value of a convertible bond exceeds its investment value, i.e., the difference between the bond's total (market) value and its investment value, as a fraction of the latter.

Premium payback period: the period of time required for coupon interest payments on a convertible bond to cover its conversion premium.

Premium recovery period: see "premium payback period".

Present value interest factor: the factor by which a future cash flow must be multiplied to obtain its present value.

Put option: a right to sell a specific asset (usually a stock) at a specific fixed price. An American put option can be exercised on or before a specified expiration date, while a European put option can only be exercised at expiration.

Redemption value: the amount of money paid by the issuer of a bond when redeemed at maturity.

Reference currency (convertible Euro-bonds): the common currency in terms of which the values of convertible Euro-bonds with different bond currencies are expressed for comparison purposes.

Regular stock option: call or put option on a stock that entitles the holder of the option to buy or to sell that stock at a fixed money price.

Return on the straight bond investment: the return that would be earned on an investment in a straight bond with characteristics equal to the corresponding straight bond characteristics of a given convertible bond.

Security market line: a straight line representing a linear relationship between the expected return on securities and their beta value. This relationship must be satisfied for all securities in a market in equilibrium.

Sharpe-Lintner model: see "capital asset pricing model".

Side payments: see "margin payments".

Stock currency (convertible Euro-bonds): the currency in which the underlying stock of a convertible Euro-bond is denominated.

Stock exchange rate (convertible Euro-bonds): the number of units of a reference currency that are currently exchanged in the currency markets for one unit of the stock currency.

Stock price effect: the component of any investment return related to stock price changes. For example, the total return on a convertible bond and the return on its conversion option have such a component.

Stock price elasticity: the relative change in the option value or the total value of a bond that is convertible into any given stock, as a fraction of the underlying relative change in the share price of that stock.

Stock purchase warrant: a long-term call option issued by a company on its own stock that gives the holder of the warrant the right to buy shares of the stock at a specified money price during a certain period of time.

Striking price: see "exercise price".

Systematic risk: see "non-diversifiable risk".

Time effect: the component of any investment return related to the lapse of time. For example, the total return on a convertible bond, the return on its straight bond investment, and the return on its conversion option have such a component.

Time value: the difference between the total value and the intrinsic value of a regular stock option or conversion option.

Warrant: see "stock purchase warrant".

Bibliography

Black, F., and Scholes, M., "The Valuation of Option Contracts and a Test of Market Efficiency," *Journal of Finance* (May 1972).

——— , "The Pricing of Options and Corporate Liabilities," *Journal of Political Economy* (May – June 1973).

Brennan, M., and Schwartz, E., "Convertible Bonds: Valuation and Optimal Strategies for Call and Conversion," *Journal of Finance* (December 1977).

Fisher, I., and Weil, R., "Coping with the Risk of Interest Rate Fluctuations," *Journal of Business* (January 1971).

Garbade, K., *Securities Markets*. New York: McGraw-Hill, 1982.

Geske, R., "A Note on an Analytic Valuation Formula for Unprotected American Call Options on Stocks with Known Dividends," *Journal of Financial Economics* (December 1979).

Geske, R., and Roll, R., "On Valuing American Call Options with the Black-Scholes European Formula," *Journal of Finance* (June 1984).

Haugen, R., *Modern Investment Theory*. Englewood Cliffs, N.J.: Prentice-Hall, 1986.

Ingersoll, J., "A Contingent-Claims Valuation of Convertible Securities," *Journal of Financial Economics* (May 1977).

Macaulay, F., *Some Theoretical Problems Suggested by the Movements of Interest Rates, Bond Yields, and Stock Prices in the United States since 1856*. New York: National Bureau of Economic Research, 1938.

MacBeth, J., and Merville, L., "Tests of the Black-Scholes and Cox Option Valuation Models," *Journal of Finance* (May 1980).

Markowitz, H., "Portfolio Selection," *Journal of Finance* (December 1952).

——— , *Portfolio Selection*. New York: John Wiley, 1959.

Merton, R., "The Theory of Rational Option Pricing," *Bell Journal of Economics and Management Science* (Spring 1973).

Roll, R., "An Analytic Valuation Formula for Unprotected American Call Options on Stocks with Known Dividends," *Journal of Financial Economics* (November 1977).

Sharpe, W., "A Simplified Model of Portfolio Analysis," Management Science (January 1963).

Whaley, R., "On the Valuation of American Call Options on Stocks with Known Dividends," *Journal of Financial Economics* (June 1981).

Index

About the Author

Stefaan J. Gepts is currently Professor of Finance and Decision Sciences at James Madison University in Virginia. As a mathematician, economist, and financial expert, he has attended universities in both Europe and the United States. In Europe, he earned the degrees of Master of Science in mathematics, Master of Arts in economics, and Ph.D. in economics at the University of Louvain. In the United States, he received the degree of Master of Business Administration with a major in finance at the University of Chicago. Before joining the faculty at James Madison University, Professor Gepts taught microeconomics and investment analysis in his native country, Belgium, where he started his academic career at the internationally renowned Center for Operations Research and Econometrics (CORE). He has published academic articles and papers, as well as a book on principles of microeconomics. Professor Gepts has received several grants from the Belgian National Science Foundation, and was awarded a CRB fellowship by the Belgian American Educational Foundation.